Explore Austral
NORTHERN TERRITORY

Explore Australia's NORTHERN TERRITORY

Foreword by **Harry Butler** CBE

Written by
Frank Alcorta

Australia's Northern Territory is unique. This slice of the island–continent is one of extreme contrasts from the lush wetlands of the 'Top End' to the parched deserts of the 'Red Centre'. This book takes you on a journey of discovery to these and other spectacular areas in this special part of Australia.

NEW HOLLAND

Contents

A Message from Harry Butler CBE

*E*xploring some of the Territory's wonderful landscapes with Frank Alcorta has given me especially fond memories.

A highlight among those memories was walking the Larapinta Trail together and without doubt this and our other exploratory experiences have developed an association based on mutual respect for and delight in the wild places of the Northern Territory. As a mark of this association I am extremely pleased to be incorporating this foreword with the writings of Frank about the Territory and its wildlife.

For me, and probably Frank also, 'excitement' is the best word to use in describing how I feel about the Northern Territory.

From my first trip in the 1960's, when some of the Territory's immense and unknown areas were being scientifically studied for the first time, until today the feeling persists. Today's Territory might appear more settled, but go beyond the towns and there is still the wild—the unknown.

My earliest work was recording fauna but it is impossible to work on animals without relating to plants. Everyone knows that, but only some people realise the intense relationships between climate, landform, plants and animals including all human aspects.

This understanding was developed early in my life by excellent teachers, many of whom were my Aboriginal friends, and led me to a lifetime's work based on natural history.

My early work in the Territory involved me in the evolution of management of the Territory's parks, reserves and wildlife. In 1980, I became a foundation Board member of the Conservation Commission of the Northern Territory which has recently become the Northern Territory Parks and Wildlife Commission.

I'm very proud that I have been a continuing part of its successful management and conservation of its magnificent parks and fascinating wildlife.

As Chairman of the Commission Board I look forward to being a part of the Territory's future which appears even more exciting. For example, the Desert Wildlife Park and Botanic Gardens is a magnificent vision on the outskirts of Alice Springs that provides everybody who visits it the opportunity to experience at close quarters the plants and animals of arid Australia.

To see desert animals in the wild is not easy, especially for those unaccustomed to spotting their tell-tale signs. In addition, most people look during daylight hours but the animals are sheltering, preparing to hunt and be hunted when the sun has dipped.

The Desert Wildlife Park provides a controlled environment including a nocturnal area which reverses night and day for resident animals. This allows day visitors to see many species which they would not otherwise see. Most will be surprised at the wide range of species and life forms supported by this dry land.

The Park is also more than just seeing plants and animals. The displays bring out the fascinating interface between the Aboriginal people and their historic and ongoing association with Territory deserts, the geological history of the area, and the development of modern landscapes through natural forces and time.

It is an immensely exciting project but Frank Alcorta rightly covers the new park as only one of the Territory's numerous other natural attractions.

Frank's description of the landscapes is extensive and I too have not forgotten their place, along with the wildlife, in the excitement that I associate with the Territory. There is no denying my special interest in wildlife and I have been in so many Territory places on so many occasions that the landscapes have almost become familiar. Almost! They can never be taken for granted. They can be dangerous to the unaware and unprepared but to most they are awesome and exciting for reasons as varied and numerous as their features.

This book provides one perspective of these varied landscapes. For those who already know the Territory they will appreciate it as a tremendously changing landscape—from the parched deserts of central Australia changing through the apparently endless sparse grasslands of the Barkly to the lush, water-logged Top End.

For those yet to come, Frank's word picture of the Northern Territory is an enthralling and accurate abstract of an exciting land.

But there is much more to the Northern Territory than can be fitted into any book - so much to see and marvel at, so much to understand in only one lifetime.

There are some people who have learned some of the Territory's secrets—the things that give it such excitement and appeal. People like scientists, rangers and Aboriginal people who live and work in this superb environment (especially in our wonderful Territory parks and reserves). They join with Frank and me, and many others, in sharing with visitors their special knowledge and interest. Our common aim is keeping it all intact so that the people of the world, for generations to come, can continue to be moved by the Territory's natural beauty.

Remember, keep caring—this *is* our only world.

Harry Butler

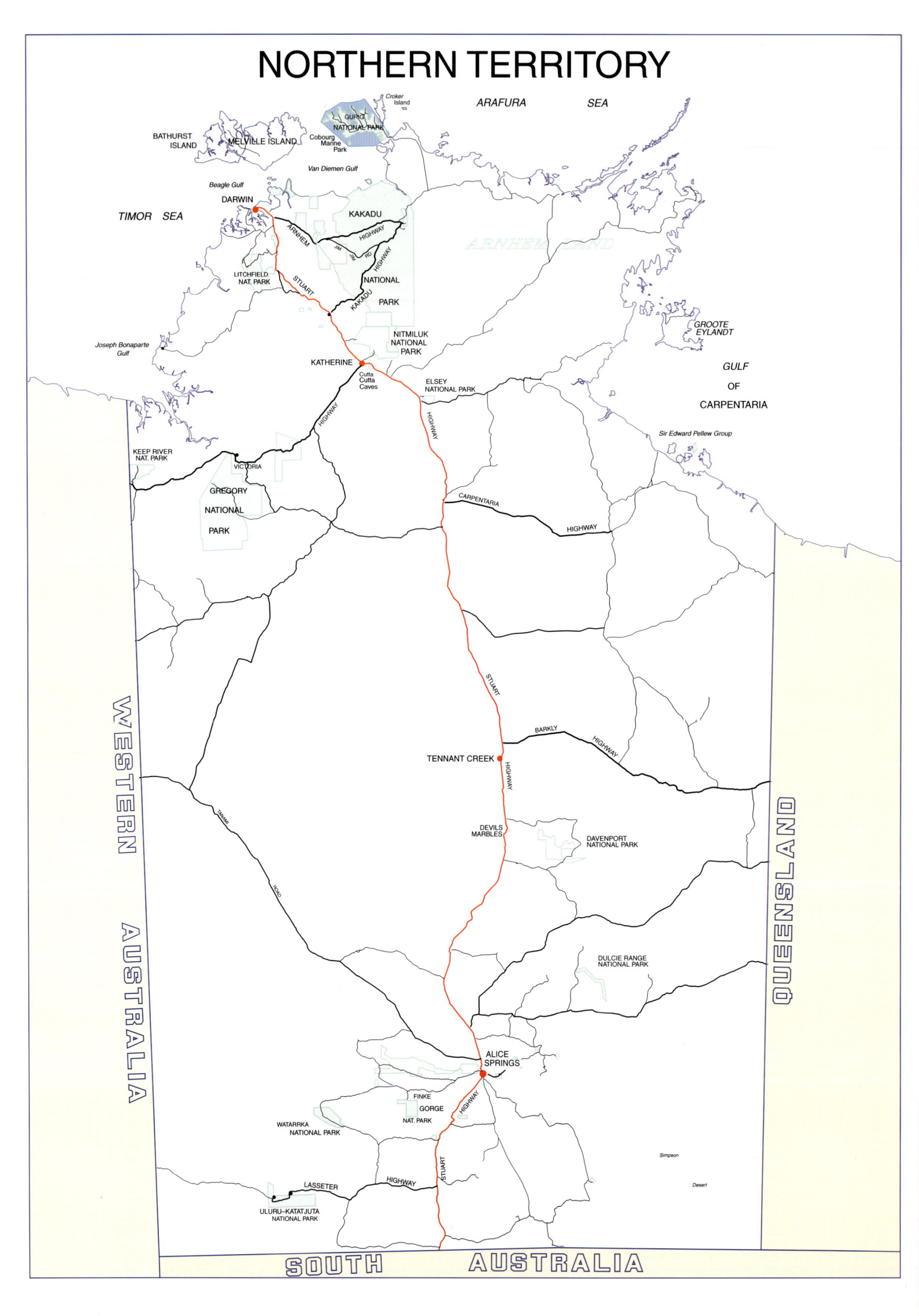

Introduction

*T*he Northern Territory is full of surprises. Look at it from the air and it could be the moon or, better yet, Mars. Red, barren and scarred, bizarre rock outcrops strewn at random like spent shrapnel, the Territory's eccentric nature shows the ravages of time and the unrelenting effects of a harsh environment.

The sun is an overpowering presence. People die here of thirst and exposure. Tourists who take foolish risks are asking for trouble. A young German who got confused at Kings Canyon was lost for some seven hours. Seven hours means nothing in Europe, but in Kings Canyon, it almost cost him his life.

Two other tourists, both young men, went walkabout in the Katatjuta region from the Valley of the Winds to the Lookout. That is an easy three-hour walk. Three hours means nothing in almost any part of the world but in central Australia they came close to perishing.

The sun, fierce and intransigent, has been the cause of too many deaths among visitors who believed they could translate their northern hemisphere experience to the Territory. It cannot be done. This is a whole new world demanding new rules.

And when it is not the sun, it is the distance (the Territory is 1.3 million square kilometres, or bigger than several major European nations put together), raging flash floods, vast bushfires or cyclones. Above all, however, what matters in the Northern Territory is the intensity of isolation. This does not come about only, or even primarily, because there are less than 180,000 people in such an immense region. It comes about mainly because of the environment.

This environment and the great distances through unpopulated country are likely to be of the greatest wonder to visitors. These aspects, synonymous with the Territory, should also be respected and travellers should take more precautions than would normally be adequate in more populated, temperate areas. Of these precautions, the importance of having water on hand cannot be over stressed. Along with taking water, travellers will enjoy the Territory more with a well planned trip. This book is designed to give you, the reader, a general overview of the Territory and what it has to offer, and if it whets your appetite for a journey to the Territory you would be well advised to seek out more detailed information and maps to make your holiday in this special piece of Australia is a safe and memorable one.

For now, though, your journey of words and pictures begins in the parched deserts of central Australia and follows the backbone of the Northern Territory, the Stuart Highway, in a northerly direction describing the vast country of the Barkly through the gate-way to the tropics around Katherine and on to the lush wetlands of the 'Top End' where the Territory's capital city, Darwin, nestles.

So sit back and explore from the comfort of your armchair the wonders of Australia's last frontier.

South of Alice

*C*ut by the Stuart Highway, the region between Alice Springs and the South Australian border contains some of the best known landmarks of Australian tourism. To the west of the well travelled highway are Uluru (Ayers Rock) and Katatjuta (the Olgas), Watarrka (Kings Canyon) National Park, Palm Valley, Finke Gorge and Tnorala (Gosse Bluff) among other less well recognised attractions. To the east are Chambers Pillar, Ewaninga Rock Carvings and Rainbow Valley.

Some of the names are more than familiar geographical features, they represent and highlight the best that central Australia has to offer and have become the symbols of this remarkably beautiful region. It is not possible to say that you have been in Outback Australia if you have not explored this area. This is it: the nation's Red Centre—big, generous, and wild.

Australia's most famous Aboriginal artist, Albert Namatjira, was born and lived here. His paintings, streaked with light blues and dashing reds, punctuated by strikingly handsome Ghost Gums and River Red Gums against imposing ranges, gave a portrayal that no one else has come close to emulating and which identified perfectly the spirit of the land. Namatjira loved this country and his paintings reflect that. When you explore it, you will understand why.

The landscape consists of vast plains and jagged ranges with astonishingly genteel hideaways and exquisite rare vegetation in the midst of the most awesome grandeur. There is delicate fragility here combined with terrible ruggedness.

And the scenery is stunning. Nowhere does this ancient island–continent exhibit its wares as it does here. The land is old and weathered. It has seen the ages come and go, and with them colossal changes have also occured, which are on display everywhere. It is a formidable land with eroded ranges, huge canyons, angry escarpments and ravines which come to life only occasionally and then carve their way to the desert where they disappear.

But this region has given us more than an emotive script of the history of the planet and exceptional geology. As is the case with much of the Northern Territory, the area cradles the world's oldest surviving culture and is a repository of unusual or relict flora and fauna as well as living testimony to the nation's pioneering era. Nature mixes with history here and while there is splendour in the combination, there is also great and random cruelty. This was the last bloody battleground between the advancing pioneering western civilisation and the local Aboriginal people whose culture stretches into the past for many thousands of years. The land is unforgiving to those who venture into it without adequate precautions.

Take time planning a trip to this area. The road infrastructure has improved enormously since the first edition of this volume was published in 1989 and today most of it is accessible by conventional vehicles. But some areas—such as the final 11 kilometres to Chambers Pillar or the access road from Hermannsburg to Finke Gorge—require the use of four-wheel-drive vehicles. Sealed roads invariably are very good, but roads that demand four-wheel-drive traction can be rough and demanding.

There are a number of firms in Alice Springs offering packaged tours to each of the attractions in the region.

If you are driving your own vehicle, there are a number of options you can take, starting with an obligatory visit to Uluru–Katatjuta National Park.

Left: The salt pans of Lake Amadeus in the desert south of Alice Springs.

Uluru–Katatjuta National Park

About 500 kilometres by road from Alice Springs, Uluru–Katatjuta National Park covers an area of approximately 1325 square kilometres of arid landscape close to the centre of Australia. World-Heritage listed, this is the only park in central Australia administered by a Commonwealth instrumentality, the Australian Nature Conservation Agency (formerly the Australian National Parks and Wildlife Service) on behalf of the traditional Pitjantjatjara Ynd Yankuntjatjara owners, some of whom live in the small Mutitjulu community at the base of Uluru (formerly called Ayers Rock).

In addition to the Rock the park also includes Katatjuta (previously called the Olgas). The Ayers Rock Resort in the township of Yulara is outside the park's boundaries.

Most visitors have seen photographs, illustrations, television documentaries or advertisements featuring Uluru, but nothing has prepared them for the physical impact of the vast monolith. Its sheer immensity dwarfs everything around, even the desert.

Uluru is some 9.4 kilometres in circumference and it rises approximately 335 metres above the surrounding plain (863 metres above sea level). Katatjuta includes some 36 rock domes, one of which is taller than Uluru, rising about 500 metres above the surrounding plain or 1066 metres above sea level.

Neither feature rates much of a mention among the tallest peaks in the Territory, yet, together, they have become Australia's best known symbol and people from all over the world come to enjoy their breathtaking beauty.

What you see here is nature's 40-million-year artwork. Uluru and Katatjuta are the relics of an immense bed of sedimentary rock now almost entirely covered by debris from erosion and by wind-blown sand. Katatjuta may have been once a single rock many times the size of Uluru. It is thought that millions of years ago this area was

Below: *Spinifex plains are a common sight in the Centre.*

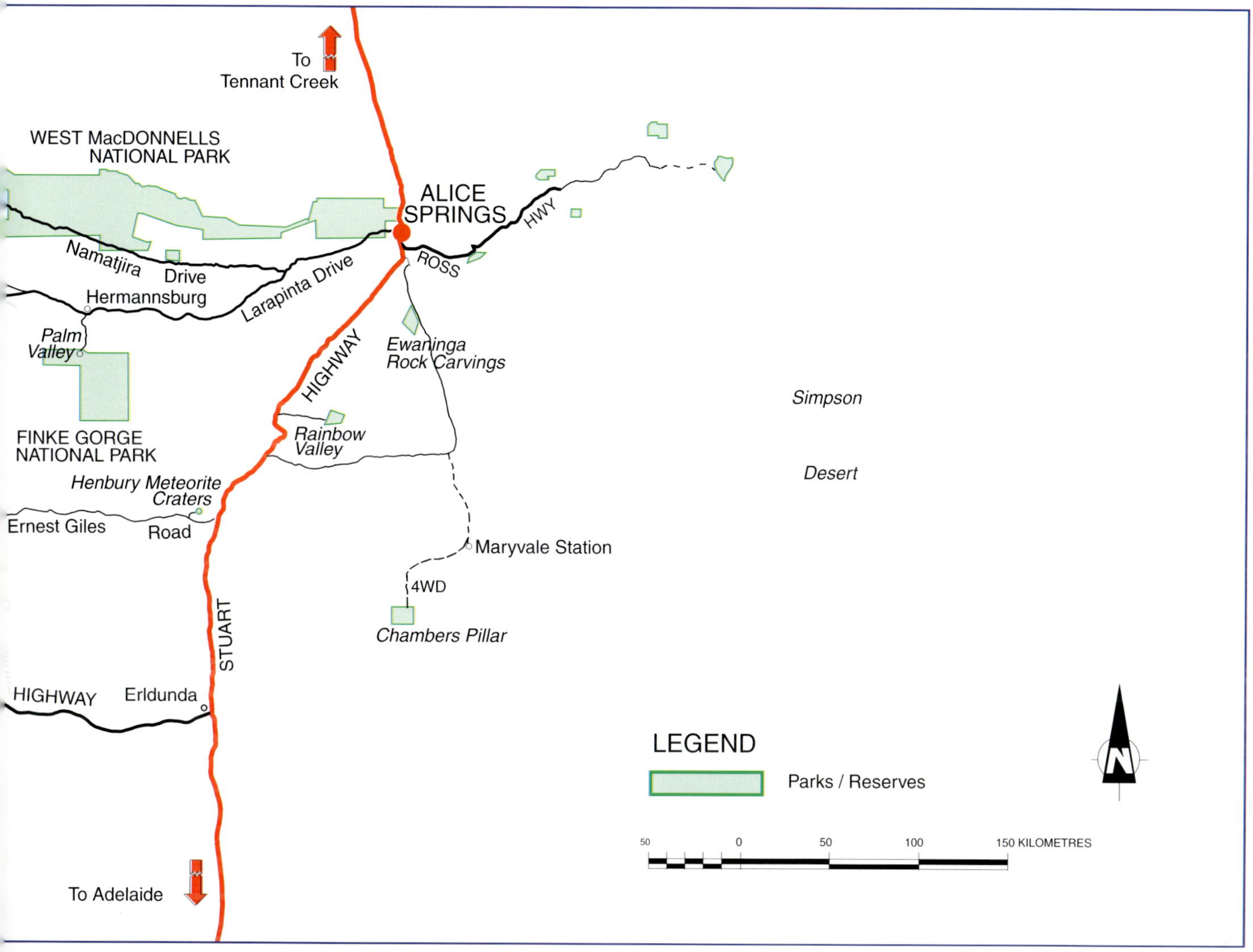

To
Tennant Creek

WEST MacDONNELLS
NATIONAL PARK

ALICE
SPRINGS

HWY

Namatjira
Drive
Larapinta Drive
Hermannsburg

ROSS

Palm
Valley

HIGHWAY

Ewaninga
Rock Carvings

Simpson

FINKE GORGE
NATIONAL PARK

Rainbow
Valley

Henbury Meteorite
Craters

Desert

Ernest Giles
Road

STUART

Maryvale Station

4WD

Chambers Pillar

HIGHWAY
Erldunda

LEGEND

Parks / Reserves

50   0   50   100   150 KILOMETRES

N

To Adelaide

the sea and Uluru an island. That is what appears today, although sand has replaced the water.

Uluru can be climbed at its north western end although traditional owners prefer that people not climb the Rock. Uluru is not an easy climb and people with heart and respiratory problems

Below: *The Yellow-faced Whipsnake can be found across the southern region of the Northern Territory.*

3

Above, Below and Opposite: *The changing face of central Australia's best known icon, Uluru. The world's largest monolith appears to change colour depending on the time of day, cloud cover and the position from which it is viewed.*

Above: *Katatjuta consists of numerous weathered red domes, which, like Uluru, are remnants of an immense bed of sedimentary rock.*

or fear of heights should not attempt it. Certainly the view from the top of Uluru is worth the climb although, on a purely subjective assessment, probably nowhere near as good as from the top of Mt Sonder in the West MacDonnells National Park.

To the south west of the Rock are the barely distinguishable blue forms of the Petermann and Musgrave Ranges. Lake Amadeus, named after a Spanish king, shimmers in the north. To the west are the imposing 'heads' of Katatjuta. And everywhere are the vast spinifex plains.

Uluru has acquired its reputation not just because it is such a unique landform, but because it can force the sun to cast the most alluring and delightful games on its surface. Sunrises and

sunsets take on a brand new meaning here. Colours acquire shades and tones impossible to replicate on canvas and difficult to capture with a camera. The sky, earth, clouds and sparse vegetation all change and become living things as Uluru provides an amazing stage for nature's own play.

Katatjuta, some 50 kilometres from Uluru on a sealed road, are a thrilling example of geological change over millions of years. If anything, they are more spectacular than the 'Rock', particularly when rare and fierce desert storms hit. The sights then are indelible. Picture immense black clouds slowly approaching until they cover the whole sky. They are not of a variety seen in mild, temperate regions. These are thick, solid masses accompanied by a regal paraphernalia of lightning

and thunder, flashes of blinding light and rumbling thunder with the occasional shrill crack of a bolt striking a stately desert oak. Suddenly, there are sheets of frothing water cascading down the walls and the smell of wet sand and sizzling rocks. It is an unforgettable spectacle.

A pamphlet that you can obtain at the gate to the national park explains that Aboriginal people have lived in the Uluru area for at least 10,000 years. In 1872 and 1873 two explorers, Ernest Giles and W.C. Gosse, came through this area. The explorers were the harbinger of European prospectors, dingo hunters, missionaries and cattlemen.

During the severe droughts of the 1930s and 1950s, the original inhabitants of this land were drawn into missions, cattle stations and (Commonwealth) government settlements by the prospect of reliable food supplies and medical care. They managed to keep their language and traditional ways alive, however, visited kin in their ancestral lands, returned to bush foods, arranged and attended ancient ceremonies, and continued to teach their young skills and beliefs that were essential for their survival in this peculiarly harsh landscape.

On October 26, 1985 under the Land Rights (NT) Act of 1976 the title to Uluru was returned to the Anangu Aboriginal People.

Some significant ceremonial places at Uluru and Katatjuta have been declared out of bounds for visitors. There are, however, several Aboriginal-led walking tours. The walks give visitors an opportunity to meet local Aboriginal people and

Above: *Dingoes, synonymous with central Australia, are a relatively new member of Australia's fauna and are thought to have been introduced 3-4000 years ago.*

gain information about several aspects of this land first hand.

The flora and fauna here are well worth seeing but you may have to be patient because this is the desert and animals and plants have learned to hide or disguise themselves in order to survive. That they have managed to survive and indeed thrive in this forbidding environment is a miracle in itself.

Camping is not permitted within the park's boundaries. The Ayers Rock Resort has excellent facilities, not just for the upper end of the market but for backpackers, campers and tourists on a more limited budget. The resort was the dream of a former Territory Chief Minister, Paul Everingham, who, against advice from many sources and the judgement of people who predicted financial disaster, in 1981 decided to proceed with a $150 million tourist resort in the middle of the desert. The results speak for themselves. The Ayers Rock Resort has won a number of distinguished tourism and architectural awards over the years and has proved an unambiguous success.

Finally, a mention should be made of Mount Conner, a table-topped mountain about 100 kilometres east of Uluru that many visitors confuse for the Rock as they approach it. This is called Artila by the Anangu people, the place where Ice Men created the Cold. They could be correct for the area around Mount Conner shows substantial signs of a glacial age. For some obscure reason this particular feature has failed to attract the attention of its better known sisters to the west, yet Mount Conner is fascinating in itself. It is a massive shape five kilometres long and two kilometres wide rising 250 metres above the plain. There are dozens of caves at the base, some extending 40 metres into the rock. The whole mountain is crisscrossed by marvellous gorges which provide access to the summit and spectacular views of the countryside.

Although, geographically in keeping with the Uluru landscape, Mount Conner is well outside the National Park's boundaries.

After Uluru, you may want to visit other spectacular attractions in the region.

Watarrka National Park

Of these attractions, none is more spectacular than Watarrka National Park which is situated about 325 kilometres south west of Alice Springs by road. Watarrka includes the western end of the George Gill Range, 722 square kilometres of outstanding scenery, varied eco-systems with important vegetation and fauna, and fascinating cultural history.

Its most striking feature is Kings Canyon, a deep cut with towering 200 metre sandstone walls sliced so neatly they appear the work of engineering rather than nature. On top of this splendid canyon, there are rock domes and carvings capriciously shaped by wind and water over millions of years. Similar to other geological structures in the

Territory, these magnificent formations have been named the Lost City. The bottom is festooned by lush vegetation growing pell-mell among chaotically arranged huge boulders.

The canyon's dominating features are its twin northern and southern walls. They share striking similarities. Both are sheer and commanding, tall, proud and impressive. But they are also very different. One wall is smooth and shines like red glass while its sister is pocked and brown. The straight, smooth wall follows a joint line formed in the sandstone after millions of years of burial. The canyon formed from erosion of the softer, lower sandstone which undercut and collapsed the higher sandstone of the opposite wall.

Kings Canyon is not a 'nice little' canyon offering tame sights or soft views. It explodes with unbelievable energy. It is powerful, even intimidating, and certainly arrogant. This canyon is a splendid majesty. Yet it harbours some astonishingly delicate and beautiful vegetation which might have been expected to have vanished in this austere land. Obviously, though, the plants in the canyon have not heard of Charles Darwin and his theories of evolution. Here lives a rare and fragile Cycad from a bygone era along with Acacia trees. The Aboriginal word for one of the Acacias, Watarrka, has been adopted as the name for the park.

Above: *Restricted to the MacDonnell Range, the Cycad,* Macrozamia macdonnellii, *has a cone which produces poisonous seeds.* **Below:** *The sheer cliff face of Kings Canyon.* **Overleaf:** *The Garden of Eden is a spectacularly delicate niche in the rocky surrounds of Kings Canyon.*

This is one of the most important botanic pockets in central Australia. Some 750 plant species have already been identified within the park's boundaries, among them several extremely rare species including the ferns that proliferate at the bottom of Kings Canyon but cannot be seen almost anywhere else.

Several walks have been developed to explore this park. The Kings Creek Walk, which takes an hour to complete, meanders up Kings Creek to a lookout point and returns via the same route. This is the least demanding of all the walks. It will allow you a friendly contact with the vegetation and chaos of the canyon's bedrock.

The Canyon Walk is a six-kilometre return walk which takes between three and four hours to complete. The distance is not large, but it involves a relatively arduous climb to the rim of the canyon on well defined steps which will take you to a lookout offering spectacular views. The track weaves among the weathered domes of the Lost City to a site which will enchant you. This, aptly named the Garden of Eden, consists of a chain of pools enclosed by high walls and fringed by the beautiful Cycads.

Finally, there is the Kathleen Springs Walk, a 2.5-kilometre walk into a delightful spring-fed waterhole suitable for families and accessible to wheelchairs.

Watarrka National Park is significant to the Luritja people who are involved in the park's maintenance through a local parks and wildlife management consultation.

The essence of their culture and the one word that brings them together is Tjukurpa. Most non-Aboriginal people interpret Tjukurpa as 'Dreaming', but the translation is woefully inadequate. Tjukurpa is everything. It explains the relationship between Creation and all the things that have happened afterwards, including the present. It gives the Luritja a sense of order and predictability in their every day living. It is their law and their religion. It relates to people, places, rocky outcrops, sandy creek beds, water holes and clumps of bushes and trees. Tjukurpa has survived the onslaught of new beliefs, including Christianity which is often subsumed and codified within it. Aboriginal people are willing to let non-Aborigines (Piranypa) into some of the intricate web of knowledge that is Tjukurpa, but crucial aspects of it remain sacred and secret.

The first Europeans known to have entered the Watarrka area were members of a small expedition headed by Ernest Giles who passed through here several times in October and November 1872. He named the George Gill Range, in which Kings Canyon is situated, after his brother-in-law. Further European expeditions occurred during the 1870s, the most notable led by William Gosse in 1873 to assess the value of recent discoveries west of the Overland Telegraph Line. This expedition led to Gosse reaching and naming Uluru Ayers Rock.

While these early explorers endured few comforts, today visitors are well catered for as commercial accommodation and camping are available at the Frontier Kings Canyon resort. Camping is also available at Kings Creek Station nearby.

Kings Canyon is more than a park, it is an unforgettable experience.

Gosse Bluff

Next stop along the Mereenie Loop Road is Gosse Bluff, 175 kilometres west of Alice Springs and about 65 kilometres from Hermannsburg. An alternative route to this striking formation is a gravel road from Glen Helen west to Redbank Gorge about 25 kilometres, then south to Gosse Bluff. The Bluff is equidistant from Hermannsburg and Glen Helen.

This park, named the Tnorala Conservation Reserve, is an important Aboriginal Sacred Site and was handed over to the traditional Western Arrernte owners in 1991 under Territory freehold title. The traditional custodians are happy to invite visitors to this area, but due to the significance of

Below: *Gosse Bluff is thought to be the result of cosmic collision with the Earth.*

Above: The Red Centre blooms with an array of flowers after rain. *Below:* A Spinifex Hopping-mouse uses its long hind legs and tufted tail to out run its enemies in furious zig-zags and hops. *Right:* Proud-looking grass trees can be found near Gosse Bluff.

the site they request that you camp elsewhere. There are camping areas around, but Tnorala is a day use area only. Before travelling into Aboriginal lands such as Tnorala a permit is required from the Central Land Council.

Gosse Bluff is a ring of sandstone hills approximately five kilometres in diameter forming one of the most substantial impact structures in the world. Here some descriptive licence is permitted because the Bluff is unique. It is a vast crater formed when an object—as yet unidentified—presumably from outer space collided with earth with an unimaginable force.

Other craters, mute witnesses of the chaotic story of the earth's past, are found around the world. None, however, is like Gosse Bluff.

Here the impact did not just depress the ground as is the case almost everywhere else, it did not just make a large hole, it created a huge inner wall around a pulverised, crushed landscape—the surviving 'core' of a once much larger impact structure.

The nature of the object remains a mystery. It could have been a giant meteor, an asteroid or, more likely, a rogue comet. Scientists have called it a bolide. This enormous ball hurtled unannounced towards the earth about 130 million years ago and hit with an estimated force at least 200,000 times greater than the nuclear explosion that destroyed Hiroshima.

The colossal detonation created an immense mushroom cloud that rose thousands of metres into the atmosphere. Nothing remained below except convulsed red hot rocks wrenched from depths of two or three kilometres to a ghastly surface. The rocks, strewn at random, still stand in solitary testimony to one of the most cataclysmic

episodes in earth's natural history, one whose ripples probably were felt on the other side of the world after the impact.

For thousands of square kilometres around the impact zone there was utter devastation. Not a single living thing remained, not a plant, not an animal, nothing.

One of the theories is that the cloud of dust and debris spread around the world, bringing an inevitable cooling of the earth's atmosphere and great climatic changes. Also, it is not beyond belief that such an impact caused the earth to wobble or shake. If that happened, there would have been huge tidal waves, cyclonic winds, savage earthquakes and volcanic eruptions.

Gosse Bluff therefore is not a bluff in the accepted sense of the word, but the relic of an awesome clash between the earth and an extraterrestrial object, probably a comet. If viewed

from a distance, the observer will see a large, clearly outlined circular depression about 25 kilometres wide. This is, in effect, Gosse's outer crater. The spectacle grips the imagination because it is a reminder of our planet's vulnerability. If it happened then, might it not be possible and indeed likely that it will happen again?

A four-wheel-drive track leads into the huge five-kilometre wide inner crater. Stand in the middle, look at the 200 metre walls surrounding you, and try to imagine this huge object plunging silently through space on a collision course with this precise spot.

Explorer Ernest Giles thought it was just another stunted range of red hills in 1872 when he saw Gosse Bluff. The explorer named the range after a good friend, Harry Gosse, and proceeded north to the West MacDonnells blissfully unaware he was the first European to sight this most terrifying testimony of earth's fragile place in the universe.

It was not until the mid-1960s that Gosse Bluff was definitely identified as a crater possibly created by the impact of a comet. The United States' Gemini 5 spacecraft took some stunning photographs that left little room for doubt. The Bluff could only have been formed by a collision with an object from outer space.

This was confirmed by a team of academics from the Australian National University and the site has become a place of interest not only for curious tourists, but for its scientific value.

Aboriginal people believe this is a place that once saw great evil. Their Tjukurpa holds that the Bluff was created after a vast wooden dish, used as a baby carrier, crashed to earth during Creation

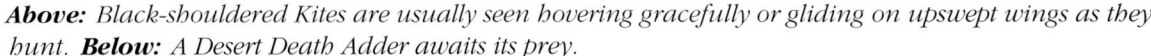

Above: *Black-shouldered Kites are usually seen hovering gracefully or gliding on upswept wings as they hunt.* **Below:** *A Desert Death Adder awaits its prey.*

This Dreaming story is surprisingly consistent with western scientific interpretation and Aborigines did not need Gemini 5 to come to their conclusions.

Finke Gorge and Palm Valley

A relatively short drive south to the Mereenie Loop Road, then east for some 50 kilometres will take you to Hermannsburg.

Hermannsburg was aboriginal artist Albert Namatjira's homeland. His whitewashed cottage, well preserved on the side of the gravel road to Finke Gorge, is of great interest to visitors. The township is also the site for some fine early churches and cottages built by German Lutheran missionaries in 1877. The Horn Expedition visited Hermannsburg in 1894, but the report was not flattering. The mission was abandoned and 'the

Below: A Cycad and Ghost Gum grow side by side.

whole place (was) more or less in ruins. . . If, which is open to question, the mission had ever done any permanent good, there was no evidence of it. . .' the report concluded.

The great anthropologist, T.G.H. Strehlow, gathered his formidable collection of Aboriginal artefacts in this area. The collection, properly referred to as the crown jewels of Aboriginal culture, is housed in the Strehlow Research Centre in Alice Springs.

About 16 kilometres south of Hermannsburg is the 48,856 hectare Finke Gorge National Park which includes Palm Valley. The track from Hermannsburg to the park is rock strewn and follows the sandy bed of the Finke River, the oldest waterway in the world. It is strictly for four-wheel-drive vehicles. A separate track following Ellery Creek east of Hermannsburg takes four-wheel-drive enthusiasts through to Boggy Hole on the Finke River. This rough track continues on to Illamurta Spring Conservation Reserve. Rangers at Finke Gorge can provide a map to facilitate exploration of this marvellous area.

The Finke Gorge National Park is accessible all year round except on rare occasions when the Finke River is in flood. The cooler months (April to September) are the best time of the year to visit this wonderful area.

This is the home of the Red Cabbage Palm, hence the name Palm Valley by which most people know this park. The palms were first noticed by explorer Ernest Giles in 1872. There are some 3000 or so of them and they exist nowhere else in the world. These graceful and seemingly fragile palms have survived at least 20,000 years, possibly longer, and their genes in all likelihood stretch to the age of the great dinosaurs which roamed the jungles in a past era.

These extraordinarily rare plants, slender and apparently vulnerable under the scorching summer sun and below freezing winters, have survived as the sole living testimony of another age when central Australia was nothing like it is today. It was a vast rainforest populated by a myriad of birds and huge reptiles (including crocodiles long since gone to the more congenial warm waters of the north) and numerous other species now extinct.

Something—probably a huge cataclysm—happened many thousands of years ago to cause a climatic change which converted this region into one of the most arid and inhospitable on earth. The jungles disappeared and so did most of the fauna they supported. Nothing survived—except these rare and delicately beautiful tropical palms in a most untropical environment.

Below: *Rock Wallabies usually hide among the rocks by day venturing out only to sun themselves in winter, and to graze nearby slopes at night.* **Opposite:** *The unique Red Cabbage Palms of Palm Valley tower among the red cliffs.*

Above: *Rainbow valley projects its most vibrant colours at sunrise and sunset.*

The presence of the relict Land Snail, first recorded in Palm Creek by the Horn Expedition, confirms that central Australia had a much wetter history than now. It and the Cabbage Palms survived only in pockets of permanent moisture. For them, it is as if nothing has changed since the time they sheltered in the dripping forests of a bygone age. They survive in the scarce water provided by the seepage from the surrounding rock strata in the Gorge's large catchment area.

The water makes possible the existence of more than 140 species of birds, including populations of waterbirds and unlikely visitors such as the Pelican, Black Swan, Jabiru and Osprey.

Visitors are asked to take great care not to tread on young palms, distinguished by their red colour, or walk amongst the mature palms as continual tramping may disturb the soils in which these palms are rooted.

The park offers great opportunities for photography and bushwalks. A walk to Kalarange Lookout (1.5 kilometres, 45 min return) is an easy climb with spectacular views of the Amphitheatre.

The Mpaara Walk (5 kilometres, 2 hr return) introduces visitors to the mythology of the Western Arrernte culture. Initiation Rock, a large outcrop in the Amphitheatre provides a perfect viewing platform for the most breathtaking scenery.

The Gorge itself is a delight. The river, or what there is of it, meandering pale and ghostly between the walls, provides a little water to Red Gums often draped in beautiful but ultimately deadly mistletoe, a parasite which sometimes kills unhealthy plants.

The Mpulungkinya Walk (5 kilometres, 2 hrs return) winds among a lush oasis of slender palms stretching all the way to the Cycad Gorge, named after the extremely rare and ancient Macrozamia Cycad, another remnant of the original forests.

Prepare well when walking. Sturdy footwear, a hat, sunscreen, loose clothing and drinking water are necessary. Avoid walking alone and minimise physical activity during the hottest part of the day, particularly in summer.

A campground with toilets, wood barbecues and picnic areas is available. Basic supplies can be purchased from Hermannsburg.

Henbury Meteorite Site

The Henbury Meteorite Craters are in a small conservation reserve 147 kilometres south of Alice Springs near the Stuart Highway, and are accessible by conventional vehicle.

The site consists of twelve craters formed several thousand years ago when a single falling meteor broke into fragments and struck the ground. The largest crater is 180 metres wide and 15 metres deep while the smallest is barely recognisable at six metres wide and only a few centimetres deep.

The Parks and Wildlife Commission has erected a sign at the site which explains the atmosphere well. Picture yourself on a quiet, clear night in central Australia several thousand years ago. From the sky comes a blinding trail of light. Giant fires plummet downward and the countryside is lit for hundreds of kilometres. The fires smash into the ground with a noise many times greater than the loudest crack following a close lightning strike. Twisted rocks and pieces of metal fly through the sky like giant and deadly shrapnel. Darkness returns quite suddenly as shockwaves bounce and rumble through the

ground. In seconds it is over, leaving clouds of dust—like mini-nuclear explosions—a faint smell of burning and twelve gaping holes in the ground.

The meteorite piece that caused the largest crater probably was no bigger than a fuel drum. Like Gosse Bluff, the Henbury meteorite site is another example of forces we barely understand.

Some local Aborigines must have witnessed the spectacle, but what they made of it is not known. Significantly, in their Tjukurpa, this place is known as 'sun walk fire devil rock.'

Certainly, the site is worth a visit although you may want to take on this interesting reserve as a sidetrip from the Stuart Highway, rather than a destination from Watarrka itself.

Rainbow Valley

On the way back to Alice Springs, about 120 kilometres north of Erldunda is Rainbow Valley Conservation Reserve. The Reserve is on a 22 kilometre stretch east of the Stuart Highway along an unsealed road which has some very sandy patches. For this reason access is recommended for four-

Above: The Wedge-tailed Eagle is the emblem of the Parks and Wildlife Commission of the Northern Territory.

Ewaninga Rock Carvings

North from Rainbow Valley along the Stuart Highway is a turn-off to Ewaninga Rock Carvings Conservation Reserve. The track also leads to Chambers Pillar.

Ewaninga Reserve is just 39 kilometres south of Alice Springs on a road generally suitable for conventional vehicles, although it becomes impassable after heavy rain.

This is a small, six hectare Reserve which contains rock carvings or petroglyphs providing invaluable data about early human activity in this area. It is like an ancient museum, one of the best in central Australia, giving us a tantalising but elusive glimpse into prehistory.

The age of these engravings is not known, but they are likely to be thousands of years old. Arrernte custodians allow people to visit the site but ask that they do not climb over the rocks, or touch or interfere with the petroglyphs in any way. Interference can attract heavy fines.

Senior custodians say the meaning of the engravings is sacred and too dangerous to people not initiated into Aboriginal law.

Wood barbecues, picnic tables and a pit toilet are available, but there is no drinking water. A marked walking track with interpretive signs will help you find the best carving sites.

Chambers Pillar

Chambers Pillar Historical Reserve is 130 kilometres south of Ewaninga Rock Carvings Conservation Reserve. You will get there following the Old South Road with a turnoff at Maryvale Station. The dirt road is fine for conventional vehicles to Maryvale Station, but after the Station turnoff four-wheel-drive is required to negotiate a succession of sand dunes for about 11 kilometres.

As the track winds its way along the highest ridge of the Charlotte Ranges, Chambers Pillar appears in the distance—a strikingly handsome sandstone monolith rising in lone splendour above the plains. The Pillar rises 50 metres on sandstone deposits laid down in the area 350 million years ago. Since then wind and rain have eroded away the softer material leaving this solitary and majestic monster column lording it over a couple of lesser mounds and thousands of hectares of emptiness.

John McDouall Stuart, heading north on his earliest attempt to cross Australia from south to north, was the first European to see it in April 1860 and named it after James Chambers, one of his South Australian sponsors. John Ross was the next European to visit the area on 22 September 1870. He was returning from a journey to determine the best route for the Overland Telegraph Line.

In 1872, the sound of hobble chains and English voices announced the arrival of another visitor,

wheel-drive vehicles only. Many visitors may have seen Rainbow Valley on television advertisements for the Flying Doctor Service, cars and a variety of other products. It is that sort of valley.

The valley's main feature is the scenic sandstone bluffs and cliffs which, during the day at least, may be disappointing. They are part of the James Range and nothing much distinguishes them from the surrounding landscape. The disappointment changes to awe in the early morning and late afternoon. The sun does incredible things to the rainbow-like bands in the sandstone. It makes them break into a kaleidoscope of bright colours which jump at the eye in unexpected and enchanting ways.

The Reserve is also rich in Aboriginal petroglyphs and ochre paintings, scattered artefacts and stone tools which are found everywhere, especially around the hills and ridges.

Camping is permitted in designated areas and facilities include barbecue areas and pit toilets.

There are unmarked trails around the bluff area and at other locations along the James Range. A private operator conducts regular camel tours and safaris through the Park.

This is a photographer's delight, particularly at dawn and dusk or when there is water in the claypans adjacent to the bluffs.

Above: The skin of the Thorny Devil has tiny channels which can draw water to the corner of the animal's mouth allowing it to gather dew and other moisture in dry-sandy country. *Below:* Ewaninga's Rock Carvings include some of the Dreaming stories which form the basis of an Aboriginal system of beliefs linking them with the land. *Overleaf:* Early travellers used Chambers Pillar as a landmark on their journeys through central Australia.

Above: *The red sandhills of the Simpson Desert abut the Chambers Pillar region.*

Ernest Giles. He had arrived from the tiny settlement of Charlotte Waters in his attempt to cross the continent to the West Australian coast. This remarkable man of insatiable curiosity, a Renaissance mind in the central Australian desert, left a description of the monument which has not been bettered: 'Clothed in white sandstone, mystic, wonderful.'

Giles was a mystic himself, so the description came quite naturally. But also aptly describes what Chambers Pillar is, a ghostly apparition in a bare landscape. It is outstandingly beautiful without peer or challenge—a truly magnificent example of nature's many moods.

It is also a significant site for Aboriginal people. In the Dreaming stories, it is said, the Gecko ancestor, Itirkawara, left the Finke River and journeyed north eastward. As he travelled he grew into a powerfully built man of superhuman strength with an extremely violent temper. On the way home to his birthpace he successfully challenged and killed, with his stone knife, a number of other unfortunate ancestors. Flushed with the ease of his success he then disregarded the strict marriage code and took a wife from a family forbidden to him by tribal law. His enraged relatives promptly banished him and the girl.

The two retreated into the desert, Itirkawara raging impotently in fury, the girl shrinking from him in deep shame. Among the dunes they became weary and turned into prominent rock formations–Itirkawara into the Pillar, the girl, still turning her face away from him in shame, into a low hill about 500 metres away to the north east. That is where they remain, an almost biblical example of sin and punishment.

As with other features in central Australia, the best time to view the Pillar is at sunset and sunrise. The great column glows like a burning ember as the rays of the sun strike its face.

An overnight camp is a rewarding experience, particularly on nights of full moon when Chambers Pillar comes alive. Camping grounds are provided on the track to nearby Castle Rock.

Walking tracks explore the prominent features at Chambers Pillar and the surrounding area.

The Pillar has been defaced by vandals who have carved their names alongside those of the explorers. This is illegal and unfortunate, and lessens the historical significance of the Reserve.

Greater MacDonnells

East and west of Alice Springs, the spectacular MacDonnell Ranges dominate the central Australian landscape and include several first class parks and attractions which should not be missed by visitors wanting to experience the daunting but majestic nature of Australia's Red Centre.

Those rugged and ancient hills tell an apocalyptic geological story. Take your mind back a couple of billion years and try to picture a huge inland sea washing over with a few bare rocky outcrops breaking its calm surface. This was an eerie land. The sea stretched for hundreds of kilometres to the area around Tennant Creek, 500 kilometres to the north. A few active volcanoes spewed lava into sizzling water with terrible violence. The sea gradually filled up with sediment from the mountainous ranges that you see in the east as you drive towards Tennant Creek up the Stuart Highway. About 850 million years ago, when primitive life forms such as jelly fish were beginning to evolve, a vast shallow sea—the Amadeus Sea—remained, lapping the shores of barren mountains under a hot sun.

The emerging landscape was cut by immense rivers, at least as big as the Amazon, which flowed to Lake Eyre, an enormous inland sea. The only clue that remains of their existence is a string of salt lakes such as the Amadeus Salt Lake System. Otherwise the huge waterways are now fossilised.

Central Australia did not escape periodic and devastating ice ages which affected the entire globe. The onslaught of ice was probably caused by vast dust clouds encircling the planet and causing sudden falls in surface temperature.

About 600 million years ago, colossal earthquakes and huge volcanoes created a formidable chain of mountains,

some several kilometres high. In all likelihood, they were higher or at least equivalent to the present day Himalayas. Then, with huge irony, over a period of several hundred million years the mountains crumpled and were deposited in the unending plains around the ranges. Their jagged edges are left as sole testimony of their former glory.

From about 20 million years ago, these ranges, in fact, have been rising slowly while wind and rain sculptured delicately exquisite gorges, gaps and valleys. This process is ongoing.

One of the best descriptions of what you will see here was given by a report of the Horn Expedition, a scientific expedition to central Australia in 1894. Professor Baldwin Spencer wrote in wonder:

'We were at length in the real MacDonnell Ranges, but they were very different from what on starting we had expected to find. Bare peaks, some of them nearly 5000 feet high, rose at intervals abruptly from amongst a mass of low ridges flanked, especially to the north, by jumbled hills. Here and there creeks forced their way across them through gorges cut deeply in the rocky ridges, but there were no great sheltered valleys or luxuriant vegetation; everything was bare and dry...'

The geology therefore is fascinating. This is one of the oldest dry regions in the world and a wonderful museum of the earth's history.

Fittingly, some splendid and rare flora and fauna have found a home amongst these seemingly inhospitable Ranges. Contrary to perceptions, central Australia is well vegetated and has an incredibly diverse ecosystem. In the Ranges, trees, shrubs and many varieties of spinifex

Opposite: The magnificence of Glen Helen Gorge is typical of the beautiful MacDonnell Ranges.

(called that 'abominable vegetable production' by explorer, Ernest Giles) are prolific.

Some of the most common trees are Whitewood, Native Cypress Pine, Corkwood, Coolibah and, of course, the ubiquitous Ghost Gum and River Red Gum. There are also varieties of mallee Eucalyptus and many Acacia species.

Mulga woodlands and spinifex grasslands have high populations of termites and other invertebrates. Echidnas, which feed on termites, are also found here.

In the Ranges, a diverse array of animals, including kangaroos, wallabies, bats, possums, emus and honeyeaters, is supported by pockets of water and nutrients captured there. Even fish and frogs find refuge in these desert oases.

Sadly 12 mammal species have disappeared from central Australia since European settlement in the 1870s, including the Desert Bandicoot, Lesser Bilby, and Alice Springs Mouse.

Several other species are endangered including the Long-tailed Dunnart (which was thought to be extinct until a recent capture of a specimen), Mulgara and Black-Footed Rock-Wallaby.

Finally, when you enter the MacDonnells you will come in contact with the Arrernte Aboriginal culture. We do not know how long Aboriginal people have inhabited this area. Some archaeological studies suggest they were present 23,000 years ago. It is possible that further

archaeological discoveries will push back substantially the date of human occupation. How the first Aboriginal people arrived, where they came from, and what motivated their migration is a mystery.

Aboriginal Dreaming mythology mirrors the geological history of the MacDonnells region. The mythology holds that the dawn of time broke over a flat, featureless earth. In this and other so-called myths, Aboriginal people seem to have developed an unusually accurate perspective of the beginning of time and creation. Like all other human societies, they have adorned that perspective with explanations that suit them. Around the explanations, over generations, they have strict protocols which govern life and death.

The Earth was inhabited by powerful spirit beings which took the shape of vegetation, animals and people. They were the ancestors of all forms of life and the Arrernte believe that their power lives on in the landscape they created.

Sometimes the activities of these creator beings are linked into 'Dreaming Trails'; special places where these spirits were active or now reside. The sites tend to be of great significance to Aboriginal people and must be respected.

European heritage here is relatively recent. The first explorers penetrated this region in the 1860s and were followed by pioneering cattlemen who

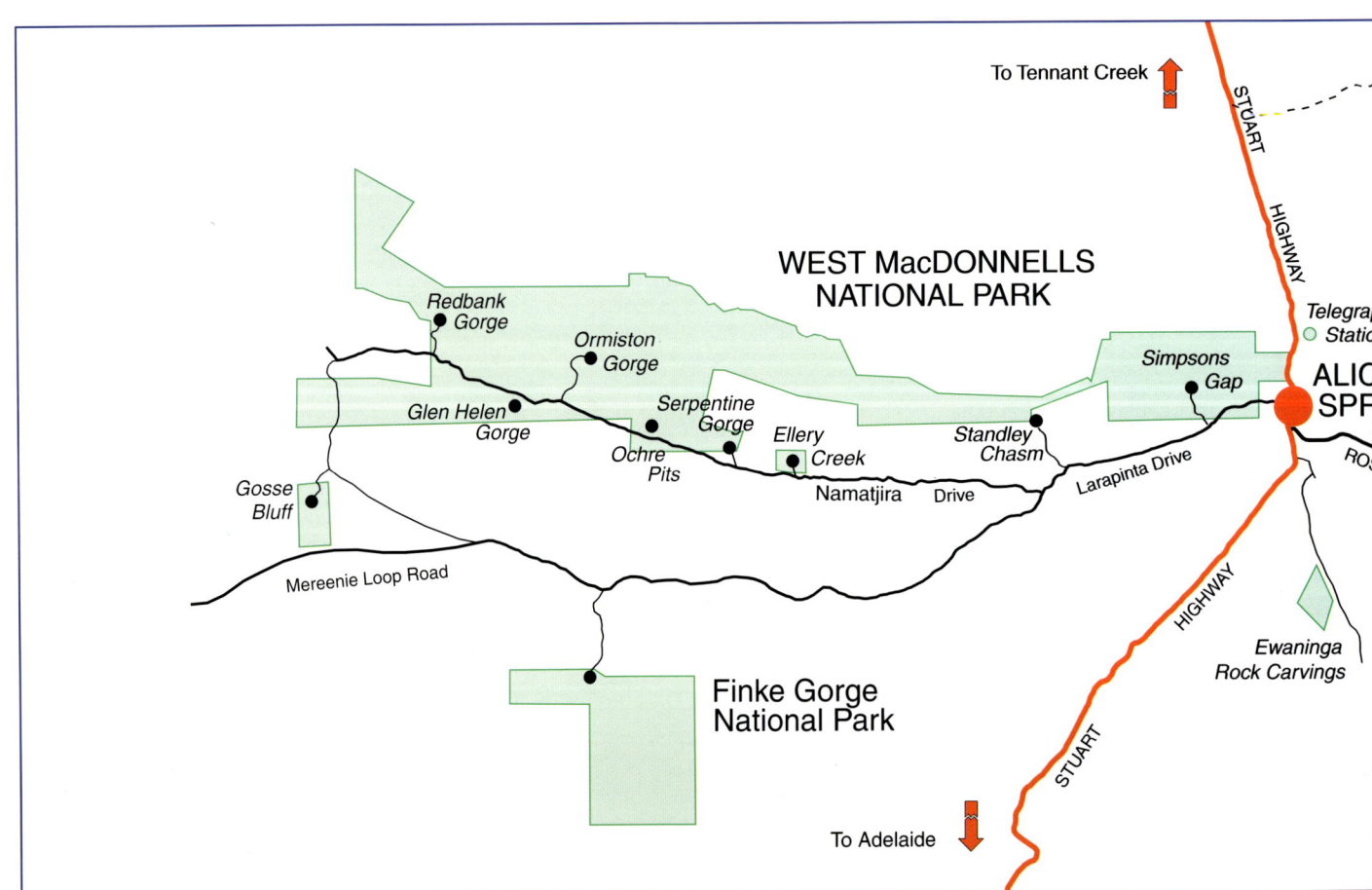

Above: *The Mala or Rufous Hare-wallaby is one of several endangered animals in central Australia.*

took up the prime grazing lands, invariably near water and therefore frequented by Aboriginal people. Clashes were inevitable. The history of confrontation between settlers and Aboriginal people in central Australia has not been fully told, but it was bloody.

Christian missionaries followed cattlemen and police. Generally, they softened the impact of the years-long conflict between settlers and Aboriginal people, but in so doing, inevitably, contributed to further misunderstanding of 'Dreaming' beliefs.

So here it is, the MacDonnell Ranges, a magnificent combination of astounding scenery, geological change, often relict flora and fauna, and Aboriginal and European history.

The best place to start exploring the 500 kilometre Ranges is Alice Springs, a charming town of about 24,000 people with modern facilities, a casino, excellent accommodation and surprisingly fine restaurants and hotels.

Immortalised by Neville Shute in his classic novel, *A Town Like Alice*, 'the Alice', as some Territorians call it, has moved a long way from its pioneering origins although evidence of those days is everywhere. This is the second largest centre in the Northern Territory, straddling the Stuart Highway half way between Port Augusta in South Australia and Darwin.

Telegraph Station

The town owes its existence to the Overland Telegraph Line constructed in the early 1870s from Adelaide to Darwin to provide communications between Australia, Asia and Europe. It was very much a product of the boundless optimism of 19th century Britons and their kith and kin in the Australasian colonies. The Alice Springs Telegraph Station was established in 1872 to relay messages between Darwin and Adelaide.

The Station is now preserved in an historical reserve and is set in a large expanse of well kept and carefully landscaped grounds about four kilometres from the town's mall. It is the best preserved of 12 such stations that helped create the Overland Telegraph Line.

A nearby waterhole to the east of the Station's buildings was named Alice Springs after the wife of English astronomer, Charles Todd, who was in charge of building the telegraph line. The tiny settlement that emerged to service the Station—later the cattle industry in the area—was officially named Stuart, but the name (like Palmerston for Darwin) never really took on because everybody kept referring to the small collection of shacks as Alice Springs. In 1933, in recognition of the fact, the Commonwealth Government, which had taken over control of

Arltunga

Trephina Gorge Nature Park

Ruby Gap Nature Park

4WD

Corroboree Rock

HWY

N'Dhala Gorge

Emily & Jessie Gaps Nature Park

LEGEND

Parks / Reserves

50   0   50   100   150 KILOMETRES

N

the Northern Territory from South Australia in 1911, changed its name.

A bicycle rider, J.J. Muriff, the first man to pedal his way from south to north along the Overland Telegraph bush track in 1896, coined the phrase 'Sleepy Hollow. . . All shade and silence and tranquility.'

The description probably no longer fits the bustling and delightful little town which fills up with interstate and overseas visitors, particularly during the months of May to October.

But it certainly applies to the Telegraph Station's Historical Reserve. It remains the original 'sleepy hollow' and has become a favourite spot for locals and visitors to picnic and relax as facilities include electrical barbecues and toilets. Guides and maps can be obtained from the Parks and Wildlife Commission shop at the Station.

While entry to the Reserve is free, a small fee applies for entry to the Reserve's historic precinct.

Larapinta Trail

One way to explore the 'West Macs' is on foot following the Larapinta Trail, a 13-stage walking trail which meanders east west for more than 220 kilometres along the backbone of the West MacDonnell Ranges from Alice Springs past Mt Razorback. Larapinta is the western Arrente word for the Finke River headwaters at the base of Mt Sonder which towers blue and hazy near the end of the trail.

The name was first adopted by members of the Horn Expedition in 1894.

This is a challenge to bushwalkers from all around the world and has already become one of Australia's great, though largely unheralded, walking adventures providing access to undisturbed country, startling scenery and pristine waterholes. Here, you can feel the pulse of central Australia.

Links for vehicular access are provided at several strategic locations to allow walkers various options, from short walks to the whole length of the trail.

A portion of the trail follows John McDouall Stuart's—the first man to cross Australia from south to north in the 1860s—original route through the MacDonnells which he named after South Australian Governor, Sir Richard MacDonnell. The stages average about 20 kilometres although some, like the walk from Jay Creek to the spectacular Standley Chasm, are shorter to allow for a degree of difficulty and the sheer ruggedness of the terrain.

Below: Alice Springs Telegraph Station is a relic of early pioneering in the Outback.

Above: Alice Springs can be seen from Anzac Hill near the town's Central Business District. Below: This beautiful bloom, the Sturt's Desert Rose, is the floral emblem of the Northern Territory. Overleaf: Trekking the Larapinta Trail provides breathtaking views of the MacDonnell Ranges.

The entire trail crosses the tribal lands of the Arrernte who have lived here for many thousands of years. The original inhabitants chose this seemingly inhospitable area because, remarkably, in many parts of the Ranges there is plenty of water in crevices and ponds which sustain plants and animals, thus allowing their population to increase to relatively dense levels.

Aboriginal people have left enduring remnants of their presence such as stone tools and flints strewn through the length of the Larapinta Trail. Visitors are asked not to disturb or take them as souvenirs.

The Parks and Wildlife Commission is progressively constructing the Larapinta Trail to cover 220 kilometres from Alice Springs to Mt Sonder and Mt Razorback—two of the highest peaks of the West Macs. By the end of 1996 more than 150 kilometres of the trail will have been completed offering some of the most spectacular walking scenery to be found.

Mt Sonder, brooding and squat, is the fourth highest peak in the Northern Territory. It is likely to rival Uluru as a welcome alternative to walkers who come from around the globe to test their stamina at the Rock. Mt Sonder is 1380 metres

Above: *Sturt's Desert Pea is a striking flower found in arid Australia.* ***Overleaf:*** *The West MacDonnells is Namatjira country, the Aboriginal artist who captured the region in his highly prized paintings.*

above sea level compared to just over 1000 metres for Uluru. But Mt Sonder has a base elevation of 700 metres against the 335 metres for Uluru. It offers a strenuous one-day return walk and breathtaking views of the MacDonnell Ranges from the top. The countryside around this impressive mountain must be seen to be believed. It is the closest thing to a broken Martian-scape that you are likely to see. This area is truly awe-inspiring.

It is also dangerous country with extreme temperatures often reaching well over 40°C from October to March. The cool winter months are the best time to walk the trail.

Distances and remoteness are also a problem. It is a good idea to tell Parks and Wildlife Commission rangers where you are going.

Finally, take plenty of water with you. There is virtually no water west of Bowman's Gap and walkers intending to go beyond the Gap would be wise to carry two to three days supply of water for the more remote sections of the Trail. Certainly water is absolutely necessary to climb Mt Sonder. There is no water after Redbank Gorge and no shade on the track.

Whether summer or winter, make sure you have sturdy footwear and a hat. Sunscreen and loose fitting clothing are recommended.

Some visitors make Glen Helen their base to explore one of the most spell-binding regions in the Territory. The setting is captivating, hospitality warm and meals delicious. Rooms are modest but extremely comfortable. Camping fees apply.

Access to the greater West MacDonnell National Park from Alice Springs is via Larapinta Drive and Namatjira Drive. Alternatively, for the more adventurous, there is a new unsealed road, the Mereenie Loop, connecting Kings Canyon with the West MacDonnell Park.

Simpsons Gap

The first attraction on the sealed road to Glen Helen is Simpsons Gap, about 18 kilometres from Alice Springs. The Gap can also be reached and explored by bicycle on a well defined bike track from the town.

Simpsons Gap is one of the most prominent and striking gaps in the West Macs and it offers excellent opportunities to see relatively rare Black-footed Rock-wallabies at dawn or dusk. They are accustomed to humans. This is also a major stronghold for more than 40 rare and relict Northern Territory plants as well as an important spiritual site, known as Rungutjirpa, to the Arrernte. Rungutjirpa is the Dreaming home of a group of giant goanna ancestors. Several Dreaming Trails and stories cross here.

Stuart, already mentioned, was the first European to traverse the area although, generally, credit for recording the Gap on 22nd February 1871 is given to a surveyor, Gilbert McMinn.

The park is open from 8 am to 8 pm daily and is accessible all year round. There are numerous walking possibilities within the area and all walks are well marked. The Ghost Gum Walk at the Visitor Information Centre illustrates the native plants of the area including a giant Ghost Gum specimen.

There are no camping facilities here, but toilets and picnic tables have been established.

Glen Helen

Walking is an exciting way to see the West Macs but your tastes may run towards more sedate enjoyment of the wonders of this region. There is a sealed road which runs at the foot of the Ranges for about 120 kilometres from Alice Springs to a secluded and marvellous place, Glen Helen Lodge. A motel with caravan and camping grounds is set against the background of an exquisite gorge and large waterhole in the Finke River, the oldest river course in the world. The Lodge itself is an old homestead beautifully restored after a fire destroyed the original buildings.

Standley Chasm

The next attraction, Standley Chasm, is approximately 80 kilometres from Alice Springs on a bitumen road for all but the last two kilometres which are formed gravel. This is one of the most spectacular breaks in the West Macs. The Chasm is nine metres wide and towers to a height of 80 metres. It is Aboriginal land and managed by Aboriginal people. Permits are not required to visit this area which is a photographer's delight. This is classic Albert Namatjira country and no one has been able to portray it quite like the great Aboriginal painter did a generation ago.

Above: *The cool waters of Ellery Creek are a welcoming sight in this region.*

Ellery Creek Big Hole

A little further west is Ellery Creek Big Hole Reserve, located about 92 kilometres from Alice Springs. As the name indicates, the Reserve is a large waterhole, at times more than 18 metres deep, and popular for swimming, picnicking and camping.

If you are a student of the history of Earth, this area is of major international interest as a substantial example of Proterozoic/Palaeozoic geology. In simple terms, here you can see outstanding examples of rock folding which occurred during the formation of the MacDonnell Ranges about 350 million years ago. At that time, the eroded hills around the region were almost as tall as the Himalayas and they lorded it over vast jungles and huge inland lakes.

Serpentine Gorge

Just seven kilometres west of Ellery Creek is Serpentine Gorge, a delightful jewel hidden away in a forbidding landscape. A scenic spot, it is home for many rare plants and animals.

Access is via an easy walking track from the carpark. The track takes about 25 minutes and you come to the entrance of a small and sinuous gorge blocked by a deep and very cold waterhole. Wading through it is not a pleasant experience.

The best way to view the spectacular Gorge is by climbing to the lookout, a 15 minute walk on a well marked track. The Gorge and numerous waterholes contain rare and relict species otherwise found in more tropical environments

and which have adapted amazingly well to the vast geological and climatic changes that have occured here over millions of years.

This is a beautiful Gorge winding like a snake's path for two kilometres. Also, uniquely, the watercourse that you see is the remnant of an ancient river that once flowed on a land surface higher than the top of the ridge. The raising of the land surface over millions of years resulted in the river being able to cut straight into the hard quartzite without changing its course. The Gorge is therefore deep and narrow.

Serpentine Gorge is the site of the Carpet Snake Dreaming for the traditional Arrernte custodians.

There are no camping facilities here although toilets and picnic tables are available. A short distance to the west is the Serpentine Chalet bush camping area which has excellent camping facilities in a secluded bush setting. The Chalet ruins tell a story of a failed 1960s tourism venture.

Ochre Pits

About seven kilometres to the west of Serpentine Chalet local Aboriginal culture is on display at the Ochre Pits. Aboriginal people still use the red and yellow ochre which adorns a fragile creekbank. This ochre has many ceremonial and medicinal qualities and visitors are asked not to touch or remove ochre from the cliffs.

Red ochre is used by Aboriginal people for medicinal purposes. It is mixed with animal grease and applied as an ointment. White ochre is a magical charm which, when mixed with water and blown from the mouth, is believed to abate the heat of the sun or the force of the wind.

The Parks and Wildlife Commission has established excellent interpretive works here.

Ormiston Gorge and Pound

About 132 kilometres from Alice Springs is Ormiston Gorge and Pound, easily the most distinctive and one of the most popular locations in the West MacDonnells.

The Gorge itself is a deep passage carved through quartzite revealing a remarkably complex folding, the result of colossal forces at work for many millions of years. This is a breathtaking Gorge with sheer walls rising 300 metres out of Ormiston Creek.

A permanent waterhole is hemmed in by imposing and towering rock walls and a creek fringed by 'old man' River Red Gums.

Bushwalking is one of the park's most popular activities and walks vary from a two-hour stroll along a well constructed path to a three day walk

Above: *The Pink Cockatoo is often called the Major Mitchell after the explorer, Sir Thomas Mitchell who wrote about the cockatoo following an expedition.*

to Mount Giles. The latter is suitable only for experienced bushwalkers who must register with Rangers at the Visitor Centre.

Ormiston Gorge is part of the Emu Dreaming path and the waterhole itself is a registered sacred Aboriginal site.

There are camping facilities here at modest fees.

Redbank Gorge

Finally in the West MacDonnells is Redbank Gorge, about 165 kilometres west of Alice Springs and 24 kilometres from Glen Helen Lodge down a gravel road extending to Gosse Bluff, Hermannsburg and to the Finke Gorge National Park.

The Gorge is a slender, narrow cleft in red quartzite. When I walked through it for the first time back in 1988 there was no water in the river bed, but the Gorge normally is blocked by deep pools of icy water. If you want to swim here you will need a wetsuit even in the hottest summer because these waters rarely see the sun.

The Horn expeditioners were so impressed with this Gorge that they actually took a photograph. But they were not happy with the result. Professor Spencer mused that 'it is of course impossible in a

Above: *The colours of the Ochre Pits are created by varying concentrations of iron in the rock combining with oxygen to form rust which stains the silt muds.*

photograph to give any adequate representation of a scene which depends for its effect upon rocks brilliant red in colour, a deep rock pool and a cleft through which can be seen a narrow strip of bright blue sky.' He thought it was 'an impressive sight' and so it is.

The walls rise about 100 metres with a narrow slit at the top where the deepest azure beckons. This is a thoroughly enchanting Gorge with cliffs burnished by the waters which swirl and surge in a flash storm, their colours ranging from pure ebony to purple red and white. A visit is highly recommended.

Access for conventional vehicles is easy and there are two camping grounds which have become tourist destinations in themselves. One of the grounds, perched on a ridge overlooking a heavily wooded valley and, slightly to the north, Mt Sonder, offers spectacular views and a relaxing bush experience. The other is an intimate camping spot adjacent to a sandy creek bed and surrounded by shady eucalypts which attract abundant birdlife. There is no need for an alarm clock here!

The Gorge itself requires a 20 minute walk from the main carpark down a sandy, rocky creek bed fringed by Ghost Gums and River Red Gums.

Redbank Gorge is also the starting point for the ascent to Mt Sonder. There is a marked walking track to the top of this imposing mountain. The return trip is arduous and takes about six or seven hours. Climbers should register with Rangers at Ormiston Gorge and ensure they have plenty of drinking water. As has been pointed out above, there is no shade of any kind for most of the climb and it can get very hot in summer.

The West MacDonnell Ranges provide an unforgettable experience. If they have whet your appetite for more, you have been wise to save the main course for last.

East MacDonnells

The East MacDonnell Ranges for some reason have not attracted the same attention as the West Macs but, at least in the view of this writer, are even more spectacularly beautiful while retaining much the same fascinating mix of flora, fauna, geology and Aboriginal culture as their better known cousins in the west.

Access is via the Ross Highway, a turn off in the Stuart Highway just south of Alice Springs. The Ross Highway is sealed to Trephina Gorge, about 80 kilometres east of Alice Springs, and to Ross River Homestead, a popular tourist destination some 15 kilometres south east of Trephina. The road is formed gravel for 34 kilometres from Trephina to the 19th-century gold mining settlement of Arltunga.

Emily and Jessie Gaps

It is only a 10 kilometre drive from Alice Springs to Emily and Jessie Gaps Nature Park, a charming and attractive 690 hectare park with picnicking and toilet facilities.

Previous Pages: *Majestic Mt Sonder features prominently in Aboriginal mythology for the area.* **Below:** *Sunrise over the MacDonnell Ranges.* **Right:** *Redbank Gorge's towering cliffs of red quartzite.*

The first European to sight both Gaps was Sir Charles Todd and for a long time it was believed he named them after his two daughters, but this was found to be inaccurate. The origin of the names remains unknown.

Emily Gap is a registered sacred Aboriginal site, probably the most important in the Alice Springs region. A large rock painting depicts the Caterpillar Dreaming Trail which runs out to the edge of the Simpson Desert. Unfortunately, the painting, several thousand years old, has been defaced by vandals but still offers a glimpse of the rich cultural traditions of indigenous people in this area.

Visitors interested in this region's formation will be able to see ripple marks in the quartzite beds to the west of the entrance to Jessie Gap. They were formed on the shallow shores of the Amadeus Sea about 850 million years ago and have been beautifully preserved along with the rock foldings.

Above: *Honey Ants are much sought after by some Aboriginal people as a sweet tasting bushtucker.*

Corroboree Rock

About 42 kilometres east of Alice Springs is a five hectare park and popular rest stop for tourists called Corroboree Rock Conservation Reserve. Corroboree Rock is a distinctive outcrop which was once a storage site for important ceremonial sacred objects of the Eastern Arrernte people. Despite its name, however, it is unlikely that this site was ever used for corroborees because there is no water. The rock itself is an outcrop of dolomite originally laid out in salty lakes 800 million years ago. It looks like one of those obelisks erected by ancient Celts in Europe although, of course, it is a natural formation.

Picnicking and toilet facilities are available, but camping is not permitted here.

Trephina Gorge

Further east, 80 kilometres from Alice Springs, you come to an absolute gem of a park, the 1770

Below: *Corroboree Rock is a sacred site listed on the register of the National Estate.*

hectare Trephina Gorge Nature Park, accessible all year round by conventional vehicles.

This is an extremely popular park for locals and visitors alike and many of the features here form part of the Arrernte's Wallaby Dreaming Trail.

A big surprise awaits visitors at Trephina. The brilliant sunsets against blood-red lofty rock walls are probably unequalled in the Northern Territory.

At Trephina, the striking mix of hues might be caused by the brick-coloured ridges of Heavitree Quartzite or the contrasting grey ridges of limestone, but evenings here are magic.

Sunsets are not the only attraction of this park which offers an uncrowded bush experience near Alice Springs. You can relax and picnic amongst tree lined watercourses near the Gorge or swim in the shady waters of John Hayes Rockhole.

The best way to explore this captivating park is on foot. There are five walking trails, ranging in length from 1.2 kilometres to 18 kilometres. A pamphlet can be obtained from the Ranger on site to lead you along the main flora and fauna habitats of these tracks.

The park contains one of the largest Ghost Gums in central Australia, contemptuously aloof and alone in a saltbush flat. This tree was lucky to survive logging in the 1950s. Many of its brothers and sisters among the larger River Red Gums in the area were logged and sawn to provide sleepers for the Ghan Railway.

Some interesting rare plants have survived the best efforts of civilisation, a few with unusual names such as Glory of the Centre Wedding Bush and Thozet's Box, both found along the rocky slopes at the base of the ridge.

The uncommon Black-footed Rock-wallaby is ironically the most common around these parts. During the day, you can see the little animals on the ledges of the walls of the gorge, keeping a close watch for hungry Wedge-tailed Eagles.

There are newly installed gas barbecues and separate bus picnic facilities. The three camping areas in the park offer a relaxed bush camping experience.

N'Dhala Nature Park

If you are travelling in a four-wheel-drive vehicle, you should not miss the N'Dhala Nature Park which is 11 kilometres rough driving almost directly south of Ross River Station and 90 kilometres east of Alice Springs. This shady and pleasant gorge does not offer the same pectacular scenery that its cousins along the MacDonnells offer, but it houses Aboriginal

Below: *This ancient Ghost Gum stands on guard at the entrance to Trephina Gorge Nature Park.*

paintings and engravings, several art sites, ceremonial object storage sites, occupation or shelter sites and sites of great spiritual significance. It is difficult to estimate the age of the art, but in all likelihood most of it has been done within the past 2000 years or so.

Unfortunately, their precise meaning also has been lost through the enormous dislocation of Aboriginal life in just over 100 years of European contact. The clash of cultures was particularly gruesome, however, Aboriginal custodians now living in Santa Teresa say that the circles and feather designs are connected with a Caterpillar Dreaming story. Visitors are encouraged to remain in the main gorge area so that they do not disturb significant Aboriginal sites in the area.

Picnicking and camping facilities include gas barbecues, fireplaces and toilets.

Arltunga Historical Reserve

After exploring the N'Dhala Gorge Nature Park, you will have to drive back to the Ross Highway for the final 34 kilometre span to Arltunga Historical Reserve where you will discover a bygone pioneering era among historical stone ruins and mining works of national heritage significance. There is great scenery as well. Arltunga is set against the bleakly majestic White Ranges.

Looking at the desolate landscape, you might find it difficult to believe that this was once central Australia's first town supporting about 3000 people. History is alive here.

As was the case with many other mining settlements elsewhere in Australia, Arltunga came about by chance. Two prospectors, Charles Winnecke and later David Lindsay reported the discovery of rubies in the Harts and MacDonnell Ranges. The rubies turned out to be unexciting garnets but by then the rush was on and, in April 1887, it was justified by the discovery of some alluvial gold near Paddy's Rockhole by hopeful and frustrated ruby seekers.

The current Ross Highway follows the footsteps of these early prospectors, most of whom walked from the Oodnadatta railway head about 600 kilometres away through rugged terrain and extreme climate ranging from boiling hot in summer to below freezing in winter. Poor and desperate, many carried their supplies and equipment in wheelbarrows or on their backs. Most would be disappointed because Arltunga, despite its early promise, was never a rich field and very few fortunes were made.

The goldfields received their biggest boost in 1898 when the South Australian Government, then responsible for the administration of the Northern Territory, constructed a ten-head battery for crushing the ore and a cyanide works for processing the mineral. These were run by the government

manager, assayer and machinery operator, who had residences and offices on the goldfields. Mining activity was greatest between 1887 and 1913, and then declined gradually until the settlement was abandoned and pretty well forgotten until 1942 when the Catholic Church established an Aboriginal Mission at the old settlement. Tragically, water resources were never adequate and sickness and child mortality prevalent. The Mission was moved to Santa Teresa in 1953.

The Parks and Wildlife Commission is engaged in the careful restoration of some of the old ruins and historical works. Information about various activities, including a 20-minute slide show, is available at the Visitor Centre.

There are several short walking tracks, one underground into an old mining shaft. You can

Below: *Ruins at Arltunga stand as a reminder of the tough lives of miners who sought their fortune in this remote area.*

also view the recently erected Ciccone Collection which consists of a working display of 1930s gold mining equipment.

Rangers give guided tours of significant historic sites during the cooler months of April to September. Prepare well when walking and avoid the temptation to walk alone, particularly during the hottest part of the day during summer.

Picnic and barbecue facilities with shade shelters are located at the Visitor Centre and at Kangaroo Creek Well. Camping grounds with facilities, including showers, are available for a modest fee at Arltunga Outback Tourist Park. Camping is not permitted on the Reserve itself.

Ruby Gap Nature Park

The next and final stage is to Ruby Gap Nature Park, 40 kilometres east of Arltunga via the Atnarpa Road. Only high clearance four-wheel-drive vehicles can get into the park and at times the tracks are rough especially once the sand in the Hale River has heated and become soft. The Parks and Wildlife Commission warns that good preparation is the key to enjoying your visit.

Ruby Gap is an impressive and remote gorge system cut through a variety of rocks and strewn with ruby-like garnets, hence its name. There are no camping facilities of any kind at this site and visitors are asked to adopt a responsible bush code to help preservation.

People who enjoy a feeling of isolation, remoteness and stunning scenery will love this park. It covers a relatively large area, about 9250 hectares, and includes portions of the Hale River, the largest in the East MacDonnell Ranges, which flows through the red escarpment and many gorges in the area, surrounded by a colossal amphitheatre of craggy hills.

The key to understanding Ruby Gorge's enormous appeal is that it combines difficult access, the elements of challenge and adventure, and a wild scenic setting. I have no hesitation in calling this the best gorge in central Australia. Ruby Gorge is unequalled. It reigns supreme over this country.

Its principal feature consists of two linked gorges, Ruby and Glen Annie, a winding, dizzying corridor eight kilometres long flanked by cliffs as high as tall city buildings broken by huge ledges, crevices and ravines, all decorated with trees sometimes precariously perched on overhanging rocks fringed by a huge variety of vegetation.

In 1886, a prospector, David Lindsay made his way along the Hale River into the vast gorge and found shiny little pebbles in the sandy floor which he thought were rubies. News of the find started a small 'ruby rush' and for a short time about 100 miners battled the heat, cold and extreme isolation in a feverish search.

The 'ruby fever' vanished about 18 months later when the red stones, which abound in the gorge's bed, were shown to be almost worthless garnets. But the chance discovery of gold at Arltunga offered new hope.

Lindsay named the eastern part of the gorge Glen Annie after his wife although it is really the same geological formation. At the end of this massive chasm, there are numerous smaller tributary gorges and ravines which traverse it. It is easy to take the wrong turn and get lost in the maze. If you are going to explore the area make sure you can retrace your steps because this is unforgiving country indeed.

No marked tracks exist although the gorge itself is a fairly good orienteering tool provided that you keep to it. The only landmark is a huge black dyke guarding the eastern end of the gorge and, at the northern end of this dyke, there is a sandy, rocky knoll with a little grave marked by a

Above: *A ray of sunlight illuminates an old mine shaft at Arltunga.*

beautifully carved headstone which reads: 'T. Ph. Fox died here at 55 years of age on 25 May 1888.' He was a miner who, overcome by despair, his spirit broken, killed himself.

The park code allows you to camp anywhere in the area and to light small fires in a clearing.

Take adequate supplies and water when you embark on this unique adventure. Everything you bring must be taken out. A brochure, available from the Arltunga Visitor Centre, tells you about Ruby Gap Nature Park. Note the safety information in the brochure.

Desert Wildlife Park and Botanic Gardens

The Desert Wildlife Park and Botanic Gardens is on a 1300 hectare site extending from Heavitree Gap immediately to the west of Alice Springs to Mt Gillen. Its northern boundary is the Larapinta Drive and its southern boundary includes the MacDonnell Range to the southern foothill of Heavitree Range. Thus, it combines striking scenery with a typical central Australian environment; it is part of the great tourist trek and is conveniently close to the town.

The construction and establishment of this Park and Botanic Gardens is nearing completion at the time of writing. The idea of a Desert Wildlife Park and Botanic Gardens for Alice Springs sprung from the fact that arid lands include more than 70 per cent of Australia's continent, yet there are few zoological or botanic gardens devoted to this unique and vast environment.

Development of parks and zoos in Australia has been very much along the lines of the nation's European heritage. Anything that departs too much from that heritage—as the deserts and arid lands do—has been largely avoided. This is despite the fact that the inland deserts of Australia combine some of the world's most evocative and singularly beautiful landscapes as well as a fascinating array of flora and fauna. Further, Aboriginal people of the desert regions have managed to retain a strong affinity with the land and have a deep understanding of traditional land care practices.

Hundreds of thousands of visitors to the majestic Red Centre almost always express a desire to know more about the region, its people, the geology, plants and animals. But there has been no facility specifically designed for that purpose, until now.

The Desert Wildlife Park and Botanic Gardens is the first Australian park of its kind entirely dedicated to the desert and arid lands. It is anticipated that the park will be at least as successful as its Top End counterpart, the Territory Wildlife Park.

A central feature of the park will be its Interpretation Centre which will offer a spectacular view of the MacDonnell Ranges through a huge glass window. To add to this, a huge screen will rise from the Centre's floor on which a specially produced 15 to 20 minute film will give visitors a unique insight to the evolution and wildlife of desert Australia. On completion, the screen will lower to again reveal the view of the range.

Outside the Centre, the natural history of the outback will be presented as a series of integrated habitat displays, with the selection and position of habitats reflecting the flow of water and nutrients along a topographic gradient. A feature among these habitats will be a large and impressive nocturnal house which will provide a showcase of many desert animals rarely seen in the wild because they are active during the night. Like the Territory Wildlife Park in the Top End, the nocturnal house will provide a controlled environment to enable people to see the animals during the day when conditions in the house simulate night. During the night, conditions in the house will simulate day.

To enhance the visitor appreciation of the botanical aspects of the Park, Aboriginal guides will be on hand to provide visitors with an insight into Aboriginal use of desert plants.

The Desert Wildlife Park and Botanic Gardens is a world class facility focussing on the natural history and Aboriginal use of arid Australia. It is innovative and exciting and sets a new standard for the presentation of this unique environment.

Below: *The Greater Bilby is an endangered species of central Australia which will be on display at Alice Springs' Desert Wildlife Park.*

Around Tennant Creek

*T*ennant Creek, the Northern Territory's historic 'Heart of Gold', is 500 kilometres north of Alice Springs on the Stuart Highway. The town has about 3500 people and is a mining and administrative centre for the region.

The area around it includes at least one of the Northern Territory's best known icons, the Devils Marbles, which features in much promotional material and would be familiar to millions of people who have never been to the Territory.

To the south east of Tennant Creek is the Davenport Range which once, probably about 850 million years ago, appeared as rocky and barren islands surging on the bleak shores of a vast sea. The sea filled up gradually in a process that saw major seismic activity. The result is an eerie landscape which—when you abandon the highway—tends to overwhelm. If sometimes you have wondered what it be like in a world suddenly emptied of human beings—somewhere where your only companion is the wind rustling against stunted wattle and the howl of dingoes— you have come to the right place.

As with all other destinations in the Northern Territory, it is a good idea to plan this part of your trip well in advance.

There are several options from Alice Springs. The most comfortable and the one chosen by most people is to drive up the Stuart Highway, the umbilical cord linking the Northern Territory with the south and indeed with the rest of Australia. The Territory is one of the few places in the world where you can drive to your heart's content. There are no speed limits on the open highway which may seem boring to some because it is a flat, straight (and well maintained) road stretching endlessly into the horizon. They are missing the point. The Stuart Highway is much more than that. This road is the stuff of history. It was so named to honour the persistence and courage of John McDouall Stuart, the visionary Scot who finally crossed the continent from south to north in 1861–62. The highway's origins lie with the Overland Telegraph, an heroic undertaking completed on 23 August 1872 to establish electronic communications between Java, Port Darwin and Adelaide.

A bush track extending some 3000 kilometres between Port Augusta and Port Darwin was built alongside the Overland Telegraph to cart provisions to the workers. Basically, the rough track furnished the outline for the Stuart Highway. So when you drive on this road you are really driving into the heart of Australia's pioneering history and mementos of it have been preserved in several places.

The highway was constructed during the Second World War to ferry service personnel and supplies to the vulnerable north, believed to be under serious danger of invasion by the Japanese. Popular myth is that the Americans built it, but this engineering feat was almost entirely an Australian undertaking. Almost all the work was done by more than 3000 Australians in the Civil Construction Corps, a compulsory service body raised during the war to carry out projects for the Allied Works Council. The Americans though made a substantial contribution in equipment, particularly bulldozers, the first time they were used in Australia. There are several points of interest on the way from Alice Springs to Tennant Creek.

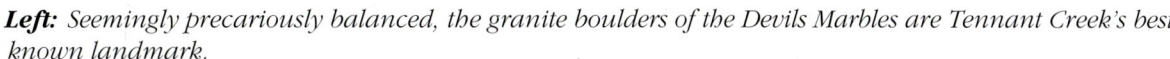

Left: Seemingly precariously balanced, the granite boulders of the Devils Marbles are Tennant Creek's best known landmark.

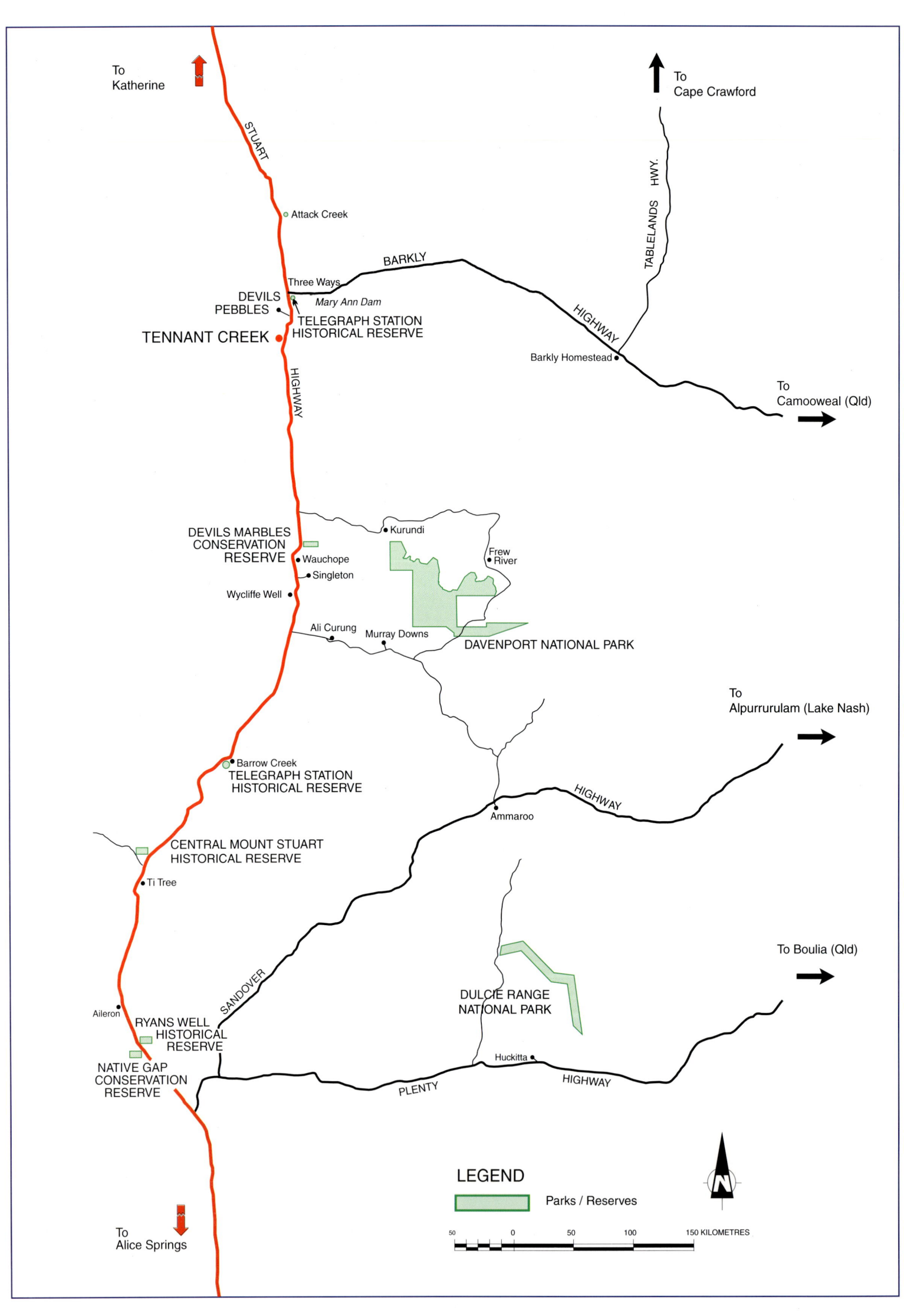

Native Gap

The 110 hectare Native Gap Conservation Reserve incorporates a scenic gap just 110 kilometres north of Alice Springs. The Reserve has pit toilets and picnic tables and offers a great rest spot for travellers. Registered as an Aboriginal sacred site, the Reserve is the place of the wild White Snake and the Carpet Snake. Both Dreamings are believed to be centred on the ridge of the Hann Range across the Reserve's north. The principal site of significance here is a gum tree at the eastern end which appears to be related to the King Brown Snake Dreaming.

The Reserve's Aboriginal name is Araulta Artwarcha. Araulta means back shoulder and probably refers to the hill which is seen from the south. Artwarcha means gap.

Ryans Well

Next is Ryans Well Historical Reserve, about 129 kilometres north of Alice Springs. The Reserve consists of an historical well associated with the construction of the Overland Telegraph Line and the remains of the Glen Maggie Homestead built early this century. This was one of 16 wells on the Overland Telegraph Line between Alice Springs and Katherine. The South Australian Government named the Well after Ned Ryan who, with the help of his nephew, Jeremiah Ryan, completed it in 1889. The homestead was named after Margaret, the daughter of Sam Nicker who established Glen Maggie sheep station in 1914. The ruins stand as a melancholy homage to those tough and ultimately unsuccessful pioneers.

There are no camping or picnicking facilities.

Central Mount Stuart

This Reserve, 212 kilometres north of Alice Springs, consists of an historical feature named by John McDouall Stuart on his first attempt to cross the continent. The feature marks the geographical centre of Australia. Stuart actually named it after explorer Charles Sturt, but the name was later changed to commemorate Stuart himself.

There is a cairn and plaque near the eastern foot of Central Mount Stuart. No picnic or camping facilities are available.

Barrow Creek

Barrow Creek Telegraph Station, 283 kilometres north of Alice Springs, was designed as a fort because it was feared the warlike indigenous people in the area might attack. This is exactly what happened.

Below: Constructed in the late 1800s and associated with the Overland Telegraph Line, Ryans Well is a reminder of the district's pioneering past.

Above: *A relic of the Overland Telegraph Line—Barrow Creek Repeater Station's blacksmith shop.*

Below: *The beauty of Galahs is often overlooked but their noisy flights mean they seldom go unnoticed.*

On February 22, 1874, a group of Aborigines from the Kaytetye (sometimes named Gaididja) tribe attacked the staff of the Barrow Creek Telegraph Station killing the station master, James Stapleton, and linesman, John Franks, and wounding Stapleton's assistant, Ernest Flint. The Aborigines attacked with great courage but were driven off by firearms. At the crack of dawn next morning, the Aborigines, again with foolhardy bravery, renewed their attack but were repelled.

A punitive expedition was ordered under Mounted Trooper Samuel Gason who rode around the countryside for about two months killing Aborigines suspected of having taken part in the attacks. The exact number of Aborigines shot is not known.

The Telegraph Station buildings have been beautifully preserved and provide a fascinating historical glimpse of an era that might be long gone but remains very much alive in the memories of the people here.

There is a roadside hotel which offers meals and camping facilities.

Devils Marbles

About 393 kilometres north of Alice Springs and 105 kilometres south of Tennant Creek, a 1827-hectare reserve includes one of the Territory's most splendid tributes to nature's architectural prowess, the Devils Marbles.

There is nothing in the landscape to prepare you for Devils Marbles as you drive towards it. One minute you are hurtling through some typical central Australian country, sparsely wooded and monotonous, the next you are in the middle of this amazing formation. It appears suddenly, an astonishing and large collection of round boulders suspended against one another as if by magic.

Devils Marbles is a natural phenomenon found only in this remote corner of the Territory. These gargantuan orblike rocks of red and grey granite are perched on top of one another or carelessly strewn over a large area.

I arrived at Devils Marbles for the first time some years ago in the company of a friend very late in the evening. There was a full moon bathing the rocks with an opaque light as we set up camp at the foot of one of the larger structures. I shall never forget the sheer beauty of the spectacle nor the fluctuating shadows that jumped from rock to rock and onto the sand on the ground as the moon weaved its sedate course through the stars. It was one of those moments.

Devils Marbles is for the sceptics and mystics. The first group will explain the whole strange phenomenon through careful study of geology or an analysis of the natural forces at work. They will

Above: *Most of the desert Grevillea and Hakea flowers like this one contain substantial amounts of sweet nectar and are a favourite bushtucker for Aboriginal people.* **Below:** *The Emu is found throughout the Northern Territory but more commonly in the arid interior.* **Overleaf:** *The Devils Marbles are thought to be the eggs of a Dreaming serpent in local Aboriginal lore.*

Above: *The Dulcie Range lies strikingly on a vast outback landscape.*

tell you that the boulders were originally part of a massive granite formation shaped by magma deep beneath the Earth's surface about 1740 million years ago. As the molten magma cooled and crystallised, the granite shrank and cracked to form a series of tight fitting rocks. Erosion and weathering did the rest.

Local Aboriginal people, the Warumungu, have another theory. They say these weird rocks are the fossilised eggs of the Rainbow Serpent which features in all Dreaming stories. That seems to me at least as good an explanation as the more formal scientific one. Most of the Reserve is an Aboriginal sacred site

Line's service track have survived. There is also a short section of the original sealed route of the Stuart Highway kept as an historical relic.

Simple camping facilities with fireplaces and pit toilets have been built at the southern end of the Reserve. You should bring your own supplies of firewood and water as these are not provided.

An easy and short (30 minute return) self guided walk begins at the car park on the western side of the road with well designed signs explaining the formation of the Marbles. Visitors are welcome to wander around the area along a network of informal walking tracks. Vandalism such as grafitti attracts heavy fines.

Dulcie Range

If you do not fancy travelling long distances on flat bitumen, you have another alternative from Alice Springs to Tennant Creek. You can take a trip to the Dulcie Range north of the Plenty Highway, about 220 kilometres north east of Alice Springs.

Dulcie has some Latin connotations with sweetness and gentility, but there is nothing sweet or gentle about this range. Here you will be alone with a kind of thumping finality. This land has kept visitors out for many thousands of years and still does. Access is difficult and when you get there you won't find any of the comforts of civilisation. If the word wilderness has any meaning, you will find it in the Dulcie Range. You will also find more than that.

This land is the repository of one of the world's most ancient civilisations. No one knows how ancient because archaelogical studies of the area are in their infancy and very little has been learnt so far. The entire range is within the tribal boundary of the Alyawarre Aboriginal people. The eastern Arrernte from the south also have associations with this wild region. Their ancestors have left many traces of their culture and life, including innumerable stone artefacts which can be found in caves and on ledges. The artefacts must not be disturbed. Sacred sites are in the process of being identified and registered. Some 86 sites of enormous cultural significance have been proposed for registration, featuring predominantly hand stencils, hand prints, implement stencils and designs of paintings.

Huckitta Station nearby, one of the great historical cattle stations in the Northern Territory established in 1913, was named after a major Aboriginal Dreaming story which, paradoxically, means the End of Dreaming. This is where the Serpent stopped and rested after Creation.

Certainly, Aboriginal people have been here for a very long time. They roamed this area during a period when the land looked completely different and when other climatic and geographical imperatives ruled. Their paintings often indicate war, but sometimes they show much more

and all natural and cultural resources in the area are protected.

The Marbles have been an object of fascination for European visitors since they were first sighted by the Overland Telegraph workers. The Line passes through the Reserve and several surviving iron telegraph poles and faint sections of the

wonderful things—an endearing curiosity about the world around and an attempt to explain it.

The European history of this area is barely 100 years old and is not particularly remarkable, for it is repeated in most parts of the Territory. The first recorded European to enter this forbidding region was an explorer, Charles Winnecke, who visited the Oorabra Rockhole in 1878. The only thing of interest Winnecke appeared to register was the highest peak in the range, Mt Ultim, about 612 metres above sea level, which he used as a landmark.

In 1896, the South Australian Government geologist, H.Y.L. Brown, investigated the Oorabra Range and then travelled to the northern face of the Dulcie Range. By then, some hardy prospectors—mostly ruffians—had intruded into the area, but they left few records of what they found or experienced.

The only other official visit to the area was in 1912 by R.H. Macpherson, second in command of the 1911–12 Barclay–Macpherson expedition which passed through the Dulcie Range along Ooratippra Creek. They recorded nothing much of any value except a few waterholes.

In 1916, T.E. Day, Chief Surveyor of the Northern Territory surveyed the area and he named the range after his daughter. Since then, the only event of any note occurred when an eminent

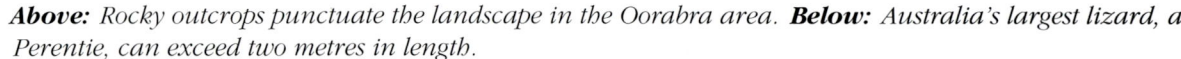

Above: *Rocky outcrops punctuate the landscape in the Oorabra area.* **Below:** *Australia's largest lizard, a Perentie, can exceed two metres in length.*

geologist, C.T. Madigan, travelled along the Ooratippra Creek through the Dulcie Range in 1937 to examine an unusual rock which later was named the Huckitta Meteorite (an important Aboriginal men's sacred site).

If you are not interested in history or archaelogy and all you want to do is to recharge your batteries in the outback's splendid isolation, you have come to the right place. Here you can enjoy sheltered gorges, major watercourses and springs, scenic rocky outcrops and the immensity of the land. A total of ten large gorges, each more than one kilometre long, and nine smaller gorges have been surveyed. Many more occur in unsurveyed and virtually unexplored parts of the range.

The larger gorges, cut into the edges of the Range and plateaus, are also the most scenic. Generally, they are 60–100 metres deep with striking entrances flanked by high rocky escarpments. Their narrow ridges are among the coolest and most sheltered in the Range. Examples include Split Rock, Picton Springs, Peregrine, North and Pound Gorges.

The major watercourses are the Ooratippra and Arapunga Creeks in the Range itself, and Oomoolmilla and Oorabra Creeks to the south east. A visit to the Ooratippra Creek is strongly recommended. It is a well vegetated channel containing several permanent and semi-permanent waterholes that remain even during the months of the Dry season.

You will be attracted by the impressive collection of rocky outcrops shaped by millions of years of wind and rain. The most notable is the Oorabra Outcrop, an area of bare ochre rock slabs more than five square kilometres south east of the Range. At a distance, it appears as a series of broken granite benches. Closer, it is entirely like one of the numerous 'hidden cities' found in the Territory and in north Western Australia, made of stunning rock faces, steep rock slopes, cliffs, large overhangs and caves, pillars and arches. The whole weird effect is compounded by crops of stunted and thirsty Ghost Gums, where a few giant Euros (Common Wallaroos) graze.

Ghost Gums, Cypress Pines, Acacias and Figs are among the more common trees in the area, which is the habitat of 335 discovered and recorded species, 21 now relict.

The fauna is just as interesting. Unbelievably in this landscape, there are fish in the waterholes, including Spotted Grunter, Rainbow Fish and Sail-fin Perchlets. Wildlife experts have also recorded 31 species of reptiles, but this is likely to be an over cautious assessment and, probably, more will be discovered as this region is further explored.

The same surveys have identified 84 bird species, with a further 20 species reported in a Biological Records Scheme. Birdwatchers will delight in Dusky Grasswren, Spinifex Pigeons,

Above: *Probably arid Australia's commonest birds of prey, Brown Falcons are usually seen perched on low branches watching for prey.*

Striated Pardalotes and Peregrine Falcons, which are considered rare in these parts. The Spinifex Pigeon—normally in small groups—Painted Firetail Finches, Little Woodswallow and Bowerbirds can be observed in rocky outcrops.

There are also at least 17 native mammal species here. Some evidence would suggest that Ghost Bats and Pale Field-rats lived in this area in the past though they seem to be extinct now.

The history and scenery of the Dulcie Range have combined with the welcome isolation superbly. The stars seem brighter here and so is the morning sky and the sunsets. One hopes this place will never become too fashionable and lose its charm.

There are no formal camping facilities but you can put your swag down anywhere you like.

Next you may want to visit the Davenport Range, but before you do it would be worth your while to spend a little time fossicking for gems near Gemtree.

Gemtree

Gemtree is probably one of the most prospective and best fossicking sites in Australia. From time to time, I guess, most people have entertained ideas of panning for gold or gems, sharing the rough life of the bush, playing nature's Lotto in some god forsaken corner. Chasing lady luck is a very old pastime and a powerful motivator.

Above: Spinifex Pigeons are almost always seen on the ground and when frightened they explode noisily from cover, flying only a short distance before landing.

For a taste of the real thing, take a turn off the Plenty Highway towards Gemtree, a flat and dry valley between the highway and the Harts Range. More than 5000 prospectors flock there every year from all over the world to try their fortune. They come to pan for zircon, garnet and ionite. If the modern-day diggers find stones, they can have them cut and posted home. Testimony to the popularity of these activities is that a Gemtree business cuts more gems than any other firm in Australia.

There are no water or camping facilities as such in the diggings themselves and people largely make their own arrangements. This tends to lend the area something of a rough and tumble atmosphere at times, which adds to its charm. Mind you, it is not quite what Arltunga might have been early this century, but you probably will get the drift.

Good camping facilities are available a few kilometres from the diggings where a displayed collection of cut and polished gems is superb.

Davenport/Murchison Ranges

The Davenport/Murchison Ranges lie roughly parallel to one another and run south east for about 180 kilometres, with the more northerly

Opposite: Peejap-Baderald Gorge is in the Davenport Range area. Below: A Red Kangaroo, a well-known Australian animal, carries her joey. Overleaf: Rocky outcrops define the McLaren Creek region.

Above: *Wolf Spiders don't build nests but roam across the ground at night hunting insects and other small creatures.*

point on the Stuart Highway about 40 kilometres south of Tennant Creek. The Ranges are within a proposed national park which will incorporate a part of the Kurundi Station.

If you are driving up the Stuart Highway you will see the Ranges wrapped in blue haze way out in the east. This area remains very remote, almost sequestered and inaccessible. However the work to improve accessibility to some of the proposed park's sites is in progress.

You are probably going to have mixed feelings about this area. The approaches are not particularly appealing. You are confronted with the terrible and uncompromising nature of the landscape. No matter where you look, there is no respite. The intimidating vastness of the Territory unfolds before your eyes and it can be an awesome sight.

Powerful hills, eroded and squat, guard the entrance as they have for millions of years through every foible of nature—greenhouses and ice ages, a sea of water and bone dry aridity. If you want kind green meadows and singing streams full of trout do not come here. This country does not have a pretty face. It is pocked, ravaged by time, and ancient. But it is also immensely resilient, tough, durable, and uncompromisingly generous. Here is where the gap between loveliness and ugliness vanishes because you come to see that it does not matter. You take the country as it is—or not at all.

I think that is the secret of the Davenport and Murchison Ranges. It may make you discover all

Above: *Australia is the last home of wild One-humped Camels. The introduced animals live in herds of up to 100, chiefly in the deserts of central Australia.* **Below:** *The Bush Banana is an important food supply for Aboriginal people as the only parts not eaten are the stems and fine roots.*

those pieces of your soul carelessly discarded in the business of living. It is that sort of region.

The Ranges mark a boundary for three major Aboriginal groups in the region. The Warumungu people occupied the northern catchment area as far as the Frew River which, in turn, marked the beginning of the Aljawarra country to the south east. The southern part in the Wycliffe Creek catchment area belonged to the Kayetye who are related to the Warlpiri to the west and to the Arrernte to the south east.

Aboriginal mythology is alive here. One of the gorges in the ranges, Inkangarti (Whistle-duck Gorge), is known to be associated with the Kestrel Dreaming, and in the early days of white settlement, was said to have been used as an escape route by Aborigines fleeing mounted parties of whites who were unable to get their horses through the gorge.

Below: *The Davenport Range above Whistle-duck Gorge.*

Another gorge, Tijirlinyi, is also associated with the Dreaming. Aborigines in the area say that Dreaming ancestors passing through Tijirlinyi Gorge found that they became trapped when the cliff faces closed up behind and in front. The optical effect is exactly as described. At one stage of the traverse through the gorge, the bends make it appear as if the way ahead is impassable and the way back closed off.

This is an important site and Parks and Wildlife Commission experts are gathering more information about Aboriginal lore in the region. Artefacts relating to earlier occupancy are abundant and Dreaming stories concerning various aspects of the country persist among Aboriginal people who have kept their ancient rituals more or less intact.

McDouall Stuart was the first European explorer to venture into this region in 1860 but it was the establishment of the Overland Telegraph Station at Tennant Creek, in 1872, that encouraged exploration of the Ranges. The first official party to explore the Ranges was led by a South Australian Government geologist H.Y.L. Browne, who wrote a sketchy report on the mineralisation of the Hatches Creek area in 1896. By then, pastoral lands were being occupied and cattle stations were set up on the Frew River, Elkedra River and Murray Downs Creek in the early 1890s. However, a series of bad droughts, distance from markets, lack of the most elementary amenities and 'the blacks causing endless trouble. . .' (Davidson A. 1905, *Explorations in Central Australia*, South Australian Parliamentary Paper No 27/1905) led to them being abandoned.

Alan Davidson conducted the first detailed exploration of this rugged country in 1898 while looking for gold for the Central Australian xploration Syndicate. His report to the South Australian Parliament is interesting because it lists the geology and topography of the region as well as some incidental, but useful, observations on the biology.

Otherwise the area's non-Aboriginal history is not notable. A man called Henty had a holding on the Frew River in 1929 but was murdered at Hatches Creek, again not an uncommon event in this land. Prospectors—as so often in Australian history— helped open up the area before the First World War. Tungsten, wolfram and scheelite deposits were mined here in 1913. With the prospectors came police because mining attracted some unruly elements, often outlaws, who needed to be brought to heel. This meant building police stations and posting men to cope with themselves and others in this utterly desolate region. A single mounted trooper was sent here and what a lonely job it must have been. The ruins of the Old Police Station, built on an attractive corner of the waterhole of the same name on the Frew River, provide vanishing evidence of those times. The Station is now reduced to a pile of scattered sandstone rocks that once housed the trooper. He also constructed a tiny lookout on top of a small ridge beside the dwelling and there he would have spent hours staring at his immense, empty domain. To keep the law, or at least what passed for it, he rode incredible distances in one of the most desolate and largest beats in the world.

The waterhole itself, about one kilometre long in the Dry, is permanent and holds a good stock of spangled perch. The gorge above it is one of the most attractive in the area, particularly at sunset, and has many large waterholes.

Further north, there are five rockholes with important scenic and recreational value, but only one, Japa Rockhole, is accessible via a very rough track from the north east.

The flora is not spectacular although some 11 land systems have been recorded in the area. It consists mainly of Snappy Gums in the foothills, soft spinifex on the rocky hills and ubiquitous River Red Gums as well as occasional Tea Trees (Melaleuca) near watercourses. There are also beautifully leaved Coolibahs in the better watered areas.

More than 400 plant species are registered here, about the same number as are known to exist in the much smaller Simpsons Gap Park in the West MacDonnells. They are extremely important in that they represent an overlap zone between central Australian species and northern monsoon species.

The Parks and Wildlife Commission has also recorded 18 native mammals and six introduced mammals, but the survey was not exhaustive and more work will uncover exactly what the area contains. Some species, such as the Golden Bandicoot, are believed to have disappeared, erhaps as a result of the effects of feral cats.

As well, the Commission has recorded 105 bird species generally representative of the region. Mostly, they are arid zone birds but, already, the modest influence from the Top End is translated into the presence of waterbirds which include species such as long beaked Glossy Ibis and Black-necked Storks. There are plenty of budgies as well, one is happy to say. Budgerigars, for some reason, have been getting rarer.

Some 52 species of reptiles have been recorded, including geckos, legless lizards, dragon lizards, goannas, skinks, pythons and other snakes.

As with the Dulcie Range, this area appears to be rich in fish and some seven species have been recorded, including Spangled Perch and freshwater shrimp. At Old Police Station Waterhole, for example, enough Spangled Perch can be fished for a substantial breakfast.

The Davenport Range is not for everybody. This is very demanding central Australian country. But the reward is more than just a quick talking point over a picture when you get back home. In fact, you may not even want to talk about it.

Below: *Budgerigars can be a spectacular sight when flying, as a flock they twist and turn in unison.*

Above: *Tennant Creek Telegraph Station was the most northerly station on the Overland Telegraph Line to be serviced from Adelaide.*

Telegraph Station

Tennant Creek, 500 kilometres north of Alice Springs and 1000 kilometres south of Darwin, also has its origins in the Overland Telegraph although the town, from about 1932, developed as a gold mining settlement in the best traditions of the expanding Australian frontier.

An Aboriginal stockilometrean discovered a nugget of gold in the nearby hills in that year prompting a gold rush. Three years later, Tennant Creek boasted a population of 500.

The Tennant Creek Telegraph Station is 10 kilometres north of Tennant Creek on a 1797-hectare reserve. It was established in 1872 as a temporary wooden hut with three rooms. The two permanent stone buildings that you see today were constructed in 1874 by the four Overland Telegraph Line staff posted here. One of the buildings was a combined telegraph office and quarters, the other is a combined kitchen and quarters.

Stores and rations were railed from Port Augusta to Oodnadatta, the northern most South Australian railhead, then packed onto camels for the long journey overland. Only in the 1920s did some vehicles begin to replace camels.

There was not a lot of planning in the establishment of this Station which lacks the physical attractiveness of Alice Springs and Barrow Creek. Frank Gillen, the station master at Alice Springs, wrote that it 'takes the cake for absolute dreariness'. But it became an island of civilisation for the generally exotic characters who travelled the long, lonely track beside the Overland Telegraph Line. The Station itself ceased operating as a telegraph office in 1935 when it was moved into the town which had sprung up after the rush.

It is now managed by the Parks and Wildlife Commission as a site of historical importance. There are no picnic or camping facilities.

Attack Creek

After travelling about 74 kilometres north of Tennant Creek along the Stuart Highway you will come to Attack Creek Historical Reserve on one hectare of well kept grounds. It includes a memorial to explorer John McDouall Stuart and the creek is the point from which Stuart turned back from his 1860 expedition, designed to cross the continent, after an encounter with hostile Warumungu Aboriginal people.

Above: *Germs Knob is an example of the striking rocky formations scattered through the Davenport/ Murchinson Ranges area.*

The Desert

It is not possible to leave the Tennant Creek region without mentioning the vast and virtually untouched Tanami Desert which stretches interminably to Tanami in the west and to Lajamanu (Hooker Creek) in the north. Most of it is Aboriginal land and you need a permit from the relevant Land Council to gain entry. When you do, be prepared for the surprise of your life.

You may have already caught a glimpse of the North Simpson Desert in your journey to Chambers Pillar from Alice Springs. The Simpson Desert is the largest sand dune desert in the world formed over the past 18,000 years after Lake Eyre dried up in the last great ice age. It is a vast and magnificent sight.

The Tanami Desert is completely different. Where the Simpson is young and shows it, the Tanami Desert is majestically old. This is an extravagant land, moody, wild and unpredictable. In the Dry—which may last years—the desert withers and becomes gnarled and leathery. But after rain, it sprouts a blanket of multihued colours. As far as the eye can see there is a kaleidoscope of purples and yellows, of reds and golds, greens and blues.

To get there follow the 60 kilometre sealed road from Tennant Creek to the mining town of Warrego. Then there is a 400 kilometre track roughly north east to Lajamanu. The track disappears after heavy rain and is strictly for four-wheel-drive vehicles. It does not appear on maps and is almost untravelled.

Take plenty of water and food with you and tell the police at Tennant Creek or the Parks and Wildlife Commission rangers that you intend to drive to Lajamanu. Be prepared for at least one overnight bush camp on your way to the Aboriginal settlement. Preferably, have a radio in your vehicle. Provided these simple rules are followed, you are in for a great experience, for nothing can be compared with the sheer splendour and silent grandeur of the desert. Here there is a hush, with only a sigh from a gentle breeze, the hint of a contained whisper.

You will need to find a rise to make camp, somewhere to watch the world come to a dead stop. Then settle down for an astonishing sunset amidst the smell of the earth, spinifex and sand. Later, as the sky dissolves in a rainbow of shades, you will want to light a bright fire.

Once I drove into the desert after a period of tumultuous rains which had created two vast freshwater lakes teeming with life. I could not believe my eyes. This was the inland sea which explorers had missed. You could not see the shore on the other side of the sparkling, gently undulating waters.

Where before there were only a few tough old lizards and hungry snakes with the courage to venture into this immensity, now there were birds of all kinds and even a few clumsy camels and timid wallabies. The footprints of a huge Dingo, a true Old Man Dog this fellow, were deep in the mud near one of the lakes but the animal was nowhere to be seen.

There were also shrimps in the lakes, darting hither and thither with nervous energy, senselessly content at this miracle that had brought life to the eggs, dormant and buried in the sand probably for years. They would not live long, only while the water lasted, but in the short time they had available they would mate and procreate and, in turn, their tiny fertile eggs would disappear in the burnished sand.

Some will survive. Burrowed deep into their cosy sand cocoons, they will wait until the next torrential rains arrive once more and then the cycle will start again.

It is the same with the plants, those hugely appealing but fragile flowers which appear only when conditions are propitious, perhaps once every five or ten years, to grace the land with such charm that one wants them never to go. Stunted Grevilleas, whose yellow flowers attract thousands of birds to its honey, help to create a sea of incredible colours—tiny specks of blue, yellow and red stretching to the horizon.

They too will disappear along with the camels, wallabies and Dingoes. They all leave after the water evaporates returning the desert to its owner, the unrelenting sun.

There is a kind of purity here, red and untainted, that no mortal can approach. The desert is not to be liked, it is to be loved— or hated.

Below: *The spinifex plains of the Tanami desert seem to roll on forever.*

Around Katherine

From Tennant Creek, the next major town on the Stuart Highway is Katherine, about 700 kilometres away, not a long distance in sprawling Territory terms but enough to make a whole world of difference between the two regions. On the drive north, the images of the Red Centre slowly disappear and are replaced by those of the tropical monsoon region which become evident at Mataranka, just 100 kilometres south of Katherine.

Before Mataranka, which is next to Elsey Park, one of seven delightful national parks around Katherine, there are a number of places of historical interest such as Elliott, some 250 kilometres north of Tennant Creek.

The site of Elliott was originally named No. 8 Bore Newcastle Waters and serviced the cattle station of the same name. It became a classic example of a township built by the military in 1940 and occupied by the Darwin Overland Maintenance Force whose task it was to run huge convoys between the Alice Springs and Larrimah railheads during the Second World War. Named after Lieutenant 'Snow' Elliott, who established No. 7 Australian Personnel Staging Camp in the area, the new township had three officers and 81 'other ranks'. War veterans who served in the Northern Territory will have fond memories of Elliott. They rested here on their trip from Alice Springs or from Mt Isa before being sent north as part of an enormous military build up against the Japanese. Elliott eventually acquired the capacity to shelter 1500 men and boasted a thriving vegetable garden kept green with bore water.

Further north is Dunmarra, a handy fuel stop and roadhouse inn half way between Katherine and Tennant Creek, and Daly Waters which was a large air base during the war and has retained an old hotel, which is a favourite watering hole for thirsty visitors and Territorians alike.

Daly Waters' aerodrome is worth a visit. Completed in 1929, the aerodrome represented an important link in Australian aviation not least being its use by Qantas for both interstate and international flights. Later it became an important staging point for air squadrons en route to Second World War combat zones.

Further north from Daly Waters is the Birdum–Larrimah area which marked the end of a long and exhausting truck journey for the troops, and the beginning of a 500 kilometre rail trip to Darwin. There is a small but useful museum at Larrimah with mementoes of those more heroic days when travelling the Stuart Highway was a true venture into the unknown.

Still further, Mataranka provides a taste of the Top End. At Mataranka you are between two worlds: out of the Red Centre and its haunting eroded ranges, but not yet at the vast flood plains and monsoonal forests of Arnhem Land or the Darwin region.

The beauty of this place does not strike you the same as so many parts of central Australia where the powerful impact of the scenery is all around. Here beauty is not so obvious. The scenery may even appear monotonous to the undiscerning eye. You have to look for it. When you find it though, the memory is likely to stay with you forever.

A few general comments may help your exploration of this area. Most of it is heavily wooded. Ironwood, Darwin Stringybark, Bloodwood, Salmon Gum and Kurrajong are the most common trees here. They shade a myriad of palms, wattles and tough trees like the Billygoat Plum which has a fruit with the highest Vitamin C content of any natural source. Kapok trees, like other deciduous plants, shed their large leaves during the long months of the Dry (May to October) to conserve moisture and

Left: Katherine Gorge is the jewel of the Northern Territory.

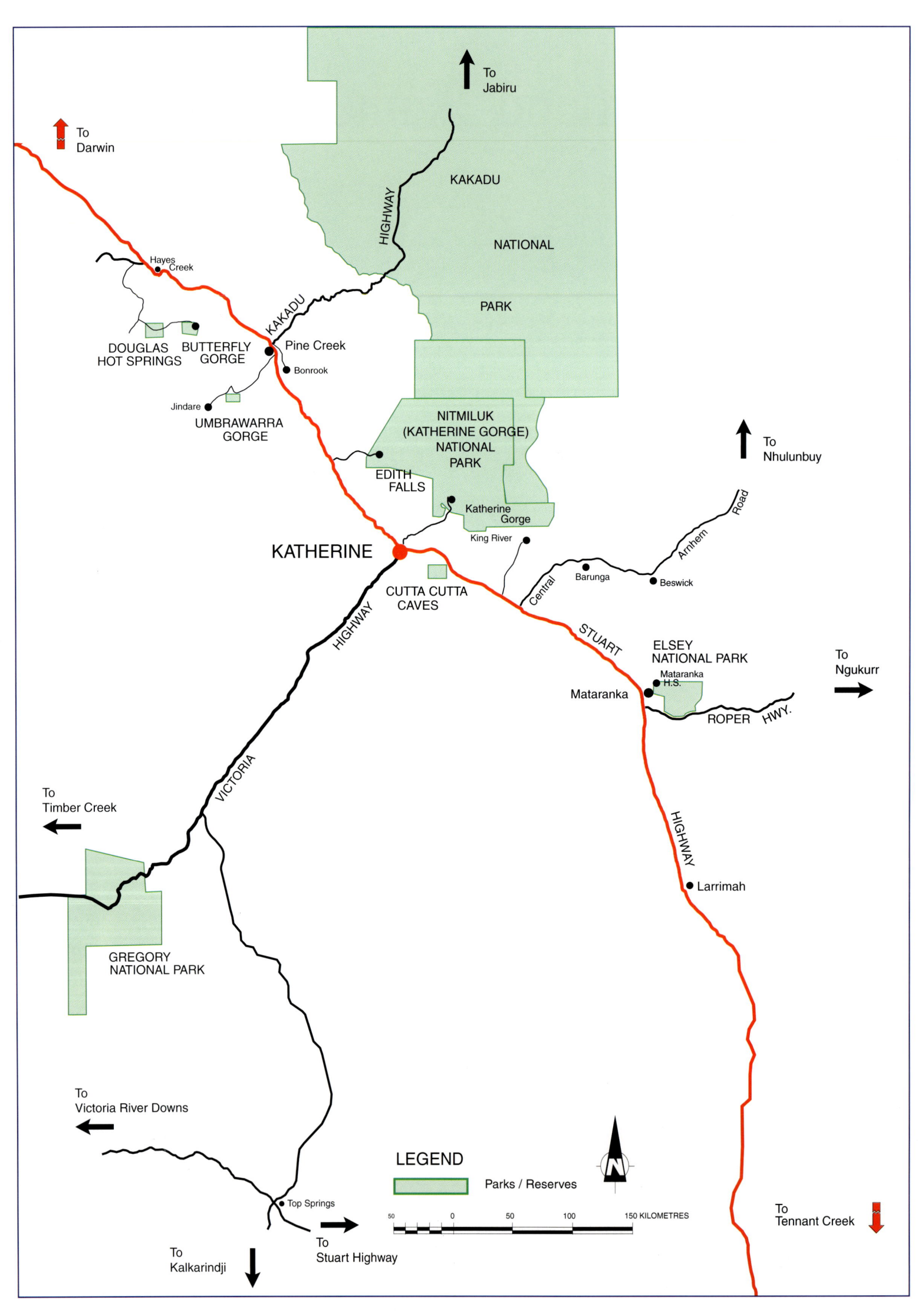

instead display a profusion of golden flowers. You will also observe Fern-leaved Grevillea, cycads and plenty of Paperbark species (Melaleuca), as well as Bush Apple trees and a palm, the *Livistona rigida*, which dates back to prehistoric times.

Just north of Katherine, there is a range of native mammals including the Rock-ringtail Possum, the Short-eared Rock-wallaby and Northern Quoll.

Along the Katherine River, mixed colonies of Flying Foxes hang from the trees along the river bank. The river hosts a variety of fish including Rainbow Fish, Ox-eye Herring, Archerfish, Barramundi, Salmon, Catfish, Bony Bream and Black Bream. Northern Snapping Turtles are found in some areas of the river.

Freshwater crocodiles are also found in the rivers and streams around Katherine.

Agile Wallabies can be seen in Nitmiluk (Katherine Gorge) National Park and regular visitors to the camping grounds include Blue-faced Honeyeaters and the Great Bowerbird. The latter may be seen decorating its bower for courtship with collected items.

The rare and brilliantly coloured Leichhardt Grasshopper sometimes graces the shrubs on top of Katherine Gorge. This spectacular invertebrate, with its incredible mix of enamel-blue, orange and black colours, was discovered by explorer Ludwig Leichhardt in 1845 near the end of his epic journey from near Brisbane to Port Essington in the Top End.

Above: *With a slightly bitter taste, Bush Apples are ripe for eating when they turn red.*

The Cutta Cutta Caves, south of Katherine, are home to six different bat species, including the Ghost Bat and Orange Horseshoe Bat. Some of the bat species are a food source for Brown Tree Snakes and Children's Pythons which use the caves as their own five-star restaurant.

Below: *The Kapok bush is common in the Top End and its yellow flowers are eaten raw by Aboriginal people.*

Above: *Elsey Homestead at Mataranka Thermal Springs is a replica of Aeneas and Jeannie Gunn's home from 'We of the Never Never' fame.* ***Below:*** *Freshwater crocodiles have longer and narrower snouts than the more aggressive saltwater crocodiles.*

Geologically, this region is part of the Pine Creek Geosyncline, one of the most prospective mineral and metal regions in the world. Convulsions here many millions of years ago caused the crust of the earth to sink and form an enormous furrow which later filled with sediment. Today, miners find the sediment profitable. It contains gold, silver, lead, copper, uranium, tin and a number of other minerals.

If you are not overly impressed by the thousands of square kilometres of undulating scrub, you may want to spare a thought for the billions of dollars of minerals and precious metals under it. Your feet are treading on fabulous wealth for this is one of the richest pieces of real estate on earth.

Above: *Water cascades over Mataranka Falls which lies within the Elsey National Park.*

Elsey National Park

You have arrived at Mataranka, tired from the long drive, probably not very excited by the landscape which has been fairly dreary since you left Devils Marbles. You would love to rest and explore these surrounds at leisure hoping for something that will spark your imagination. Here, you will not be disappointed.

The 13,000 hectare Elsey National Park, 110 kilometres south of Katherine, offers great scenery, a relaxed bush camping holiday, fishing, swimming, canoeing, walking or simply putting your feet up and doing nothing at all.

The park includes Elsey Station, the 19th century home of pastoralist Aeneas Gunn and his author wife, Jeannie, who immortalised those pioneering days with her classic book, *'We of the Never Never'*.

The historic Elsey Cemetery, 20 kilometres south of Mataranka on the original Stuart Highway, is believed to contain the remains of some of the characters featured in the book although they have not been identified.

This area therefore is of great importance to European Territorians for its links with the Territory's pioneering past. It is also very important to the Yangman–Mangari traditional owners. There are several sacred sites of great significance—indeed all mature paperbark trees are sacred to these Aboriginal people who are the direct descendants of those who have been immortalised in *'We of the Never Never'*.

Central to the park is its best known feature, the Mataranka Thermal Springs. The terrain around the Springs tends to be monotonous and predictable—dusty savannah country dotted with trees crying for water. Among this is an oasis of tall and luxuriant palms surrounding pools of clear water. The thermal pools are much cooler than those you will find further north at Douglas Hot Springs and thousands of people visit every year to bathe and frolic in comfort. The Mataranka Thermal Pool Nature Park is managed by the Parks and Wildlife Commission.

Adjacent to the park is a private venture, the Mataranka Homestead which provides excellent camping facilities, caravan sites, and limited motel accommodation. The same firm also has a restaurant and runs a bar and souvenir shop.

The pools have been formed by a leakage of artesian water from the saturated limestone beneath the surface. A formidable maze of cracks, tunnels and caves riddles the limestone beds which lie between 30 and 100 metres below the surface. Some of the torrential water that falls during the wet season trickles down into the maze and, at this depth, is heated to a temperature which rarely, if ever, goes above 34°C. The water flows to a gradient towards the upper reaches of the Roper River nearby. A fracture in the rock

layers over the limestone at Mataranka has allowed water to escape.

The pools are a popular destination which will continue to attract large numbers of visitors. The same applies to the rest of the park. It is easy to reach, has good camping facilities and offers a great bush experience without the hassles sometimes associated with driving to a remote area.

It is also a birdwatcher's paradise. The park's abundant birdlife includes majestic raptors, parrots, finches, honeyeaters, flycatchers and the fascinating Apostle Bird, so named because of its apparent propensity to gather in groups of 12.

Visitors will also be fascinated by the colourful tufa formations in sections of the Roper River which flows sedately through the park. These delicate limestone structures are extraordinarily fragile and have created natural dams of crystal clear water attractive to swimmers who should take care not to damage them. The tufas tend to crumble when treated roughly. The most significant of these formations is at Mataranka Falls on the park's eastern edge, where a considerable bar of limestone has built up.

John Hauser Drive, named after a long serving Territory forester, leads off the access road to the Mataranka Thermal Springs and, through the park, to the Roper Highway. It is located approximately 1500 metres from the banks of the Upper Roper, far enough to ensure that campers are not disturbed by the traffic and that the ecology of the area remains protected.

Above: *Red-backed Kingfishers can be found throughout the Northern Territory.*

Left: *The crystal clear waters of Mataranka Thermal Springs are a welcome haven for visitors.*
Below: *Bushwalking in the Northern region can offer secluded spots like this one known as Sweet Water.*
Overleaf: *Near Mataranka, this area in Elsey National Park is called Mulurark.*

The park is superbly scenic. It includes magnificent flora, particularly the distinctive Pandanus stands near the Roper River, and fauna. It also has great cultural value not only for its Aboriginal content but also for those interested in more recent history. For example, the Territory's first Administrator, Dr John Anderson Gilruth (1911–19), built a sheep dip here, still in good condition, just south of the main access road. Also, the Upper Roper was traversed by several European explorers. Leichhardt, on his journey from near Brisbane to Port Essington, in fact named the river and John McDouall Stuart later named the Waterhouse as well as Katherine Rivers.

Elsey has been well and truly discovered, although at least at this stage you are not likely to find it over crowded. Certainly for visitors driving from Tennant Creek, this park comes as a delightful surprise. It is an oasis in the middle of nowhere offering a chance to relax, rest, and maybe do some canoeing or fishing.

A well equipped camping area has been established at the historic 12 Mile Yards site and provides hot showers, toilets, laundry troughs and a kiosk. Pontoons have been placed in an adjacent stretch of the river to provide easy access and a pleasant resting platform for swimmers. Two nearby special day-use areas have on-site barbecues, tables and seating, and easy access to walking trails.

Several walking tracks provide access to the park's rich wilderness attractions. Rangers usually conduct guided tours during the dry season designed to allow visitors to fully appreciate Elsey's diverse wildlife.

One park-based concessionaire has canoes available for hire. Another private operator offers horseback rides for visitors through peaceful bushland that has changed little from the pioneering days.

Cutta Cutta Caves

Just up the road from Mataranka is the 1500 hectare Cutta Cutta Caves Nature Park, 30 kilometres south of Katherine off the Stuart Highway. This park includes a spectacular and extensive limestone cave system with karst (limestone) outcrops. The area contains one of the largest limestone deposits in Australia stretching 100 kilometres by 20 kilometres.

The description is accurate but might not excite your mind. Try to picture this area another way. If you are curious to know how the Great Barrier Reef may look in, say, 500 million years, come to Cutta Cutta Caves. That is what this place was, another Great Barrier Reef submerged under stormy seas and teeming with marine life. The seas have long receded, the marine life perished (except for a tough little shrimp that lives a blind existence in

relatively cool water at the deep end of the caves), and the live algae have given way to carbeen gums, small-leaf bauhinia and some relic species of fig surrounded by tall tropical monsoon grasses.

But the sheer adventure of geology persists, for here you witness the colossal change that slowly shaped northern Australia. About 500 million years ago this striking formation was indeed a barrier reef fringed by white sandy beaches and tropical rainforest. Patches of the rainforest that covered not just this area but much of the Top End can still be found here

preserved by limestone firebreaks. One is adjacent to Cutta Cutta Caves.

The sea withdrew and, in time, left behind a karst landscape associated with the Tindall limestone. What happened since then is the product of erosion. It caused limestone to assume unusual structures such as weirdly carved towers or huge caves. The caves are the result of rain reacting with the limestone and dissolving it until large masses collapse or implode.

Cutta Cutta itself is an example of such a collapse. It is the only developed cave in the Northern Territory and contains fauna rarely found elsewhere. The cave was named Smiths before the Second World War, after a stockilometrean who stumbled upon it by chance in 1900. During the war, when thousands of soldiers were stationed in this area, the name was changed to Sixteen Mile Cave.

The Aboriginal people here of course knew of its existence but avoided it, apparently because they believed the cave was the home of evil spirits. They were not far off the mark. Here lives the uncommon Ghost Bat which

Below: *Brown Tree Snakes are spectacular climbers with the ability to hold most of their bodies in the air as they move from tree to tree.*

can reach a span of almost one metre and really looks like something out of a horror film. You will be lucky to see one because they are shy creatures.

Australia's largest cave-dwelling bat, Ghost Bats eat small mammals, reptiles, birds and other bats. There is no shortage of food for these bats in Cutta Cutta which is also the home of another uncommon bat, the Orange Horseshoe Bat which is found in only a handful of Top End locations.

There is also a number of tree snakes inside. In fact, this is one of the very few places where visitors are likely to see snakes in the wild. The tree snake you find here is a beautiful brown and white banded reptile extremely proficient at climbing the smooth cave walls. The species breeds in the caves during the wet season. They are venomous but their fangs are positioned at the rear of their mouths which makes them incapable of taking a good bite and are therefore judged inoffensive.

Snakes and bats provide a perfect background for the spectacular scene inside. Stalactites reach down from the ceiling, ever so gradually approaching stalagmites rising up from the floor to form columns of inimitable grace. They are not in

a hurry either. This construction site has been busy for many thousands of years and will go on for many thousands more.

A byzantine cathedral of colours and shades, of inexplicable forms and strange shapes, greets the eye as the cave goes deeper into the earth. Calcite crystals and aragonites make the walls sparkle as if peppered with tiny diamonds.

Beyond the tastefully lit and well developed section is the entrance to another less orderly and civilised world, one utterly dark and silent. And it is here that the blind shrimp lives.

The shrimp (previously unrecorded in Australia) is an almost extinct relic of an ancient creature and swims in pools deep in the cave. The only other place it has been found is on the island of Madagascar providing, perhaps, another piece of evidence in favour of continental drift. This little animal is a determined survivor. It cannot see because it has no eyes and no pigment to colour its dark world. But it has survived since the Cambrian period. No other animal, not even that other great Top End survivor, the crocodile, can claim a more ancient lineage.

Other cave tours complement Cutta Cutta and make this nature park even more attractive and interesting. Tindall Cave is an added attraction on

Left: *This intriguing formation is typical of Cutta Cutta Caves.* **Below:** *Frilled Lizards display their magnificent neck frills when alarmed.*

the park which features an interesting surface walk through amazing karst towers and labyrinths of limestone.

Also, for visitors who prefer to stay above ground, there is a series of attractive walking trails which meander through the park's open woodland.

The caves are occasionally closed during the wet season because potential flooding can make electric lighting hazardous.

Concessionaire-operated cave tours are in place at modest charges. There are no camping facilities but toilets and parking are available.

Nitmiluk (Katherine Gorge)

From Cutta Cutta it is a short drive to Katherine and, just 32 kilometres north east of the town centre, to Nitmiluk (Katherine Gorge) National Park, one of the most visited and best recognised Territory landmarks. For the purposes of tourism and conservation, Nitmiluk includes Edith Falls to the north of Katherine, but I prefer to consider them separately because Edith is a special place which deserves a special mention.

The 300,000 hectare park, now owned by its Jawoyn traditional owners and jointly managed with the Parks and Wildlife Commission, consists

Left: The Top End variety of Rainbow Lorikeets and Red-collared Lorikeets travel in flocks searching for flowers and fruit. *Above:* Flowering Eucalypts are a source of colour in the Top End bush. *Below:* The Northern Quoll is sometimes called the Native Cat but it is a marsupial and no relation to the domestic cat. *Overleaf:* The spectacular high walls and deep blue waters of Katherine Gorge attract thousands of visitors each year.

Above: *Cycads are a beautiful feature of the Top End bush. Although sometimes referred to as palms, Cycads are not related to palms.* **Right:** *Biddlecombe Cascades make a picturesque stop-over point for bushwalkers trekking through Nitmiluk National Park.*

of 13 splendid gorges which offer a scenic wonder, safe swimming, canoeing, bushwalking, photography and Aboriginal art sites. Or you can do the sensible thing: sit back and relax while a boat takes you for a cruise amongst the towering red cliffs.

The whole experience really has to do with a fantastic trip into earth's earliest history. Katherine Gorge began to be formed about 1400 to 1800 million years ago. These rocks were shaped before primitive life appeared on earth and they have been washed clean by aeons of climatic changes. Long, long before man came, these red cliffs had grown old.

This has been a hunting and gathering region for the Jawoyn as they and the Dagoman were the landlords until Europeans arrived. The Dagoman have dwindled but the Jawoyn have managed to retain a strong cultural and physical presence in the Katherine region.

The presence of their ancestors is evident in many superb samples of rock art which can be found throughout the park. Many of the paintings depict important native fauna and hunting scenes. Others tell the stories of Jawoyn Dreaming ancestors.

Bush walkers in Nitmiluk might come across evidence of Aboriginal ceremonial use of the area in the form of parallel arrangements of stones in places along the way.

European history here is quite recent. Although the Katherine River, which feeds the Gorge, was first discovered by Leichhardt in 1844, it was named by South Australian explorer, McDouall Stuart, on 4 July 1862, after Catherine, the daughter of his patron, James Chambers. There is no record that either of the two explorers actually saw the Gorge itself.

In fact it is not known who was the first European to discover Katherine Gorge. It could not have been Stuart because he crossed the river some 80 kilometres upstream from Katherine. Leichhardt, a man of insatiable curiosity, may well have caught a glimpse, but he wrote nothing about it and spoke to no one about the discovery which would have been significant.

Another explorer, David Lindsay, followed the river in 1833 until the terrain got too rugged forcing him to cut across country to the familiar landmark of the Overland Telegraph. If this record is accurate, Lindsay would have come within five or six kilometres of the first and

second gorges, not close enough to see them. After him there were cattlemen, missionaries, traders, prospectors, ruffians and adventurers, but no single outstanding personality to whom the discovery can be credited although it is widely believed that Alfred Giles, the manager of nearby Springvale Station and an experienced bushman, was the first European to sight the entrance to the first gorge in what is now Nitmiluk (Katherine Gorge) National Park.

The flora here is diverse and contains at least six endangered species, including a wattle species endemic to the Nitmiluk area. Monsoon rainforests grow in the park's sheltered ravines. This diversity is featured in plateaus, open woodlands and riverine habitats. Darwin Woollybutts, Fan-leafed Bloodwoods, River Red Gums and Salmon Gums can also be found.

The fauna is just as varied including Barramundi in the waterways, turtles, water monitors, Freshwater Long Tom and a number of Bream species as well as freshwater crocodiles. There are also 168 species of birds including darters, Little Pied Cormorants and Little Black Cormorants. Gouldian Finches and Hooded Parrots are also significant residents of this Park.

Walkers are well catered for by an excellent network of signposted trails. The most popular short bush walks include those to Lily Ponds, Smitt's Rock and Butterfly Gorge.

Crystal Falls, about 25 kilometres north of the gorge itself, while not as spectacular, is even more beautiful. As its name indicates, it consists of a 30 metre crystal clear waterfall fully surrounded by rainforest. It is difficult to believe a place like this can exist in an otherwise semi-arid environment.

The walk to Crystal Falls takes about a day and a half. The track, marked with blue and white trail markers, leads first to Biddlecombe Cascades where, as well as a creek and rockhole escarpment, there are some striking Aboriginal rock arrangements. The best time of the year for the walk, which extends from Crystal Falls to 17 Mile Falls and ends in Edith Falls 76 kilometres away, is from April to the end of September when sunny days and cool nights prevail.

Bushwalkers should wear sturdy shoes and hats. Take plenty of water as well although Biddlecombe and Crystal Falls carry good quality water even during the dry season.

Walking this track, particularly if followed all the way to Edith Falls, requires a map which may be obtained from the Visitor Centre for a small fee.

In all, Commission rangers have developed four tracks for a total of more than 100 kilometres as well as six one day walks. Visitors who intend to take a camping trek must report to the Visitor Centre and obtain a permit. This enables Rangers to organise a search if you fail to arrive at your destination by the due date.

This is ideal country for camera work. From Crystal Falls the view across a huge chasm, which begins at 17 Mile Falls and ends south of Katherine Gorge, is stunning. The chasm's origins have not been fully determined, but it looks like a reservoir which once probably was a vast lake or immensely wide river. All that is left is the Katherine River, puny in comparison but vital to Katherine's inhabitants who get their water from this river.

Facilities here are very good. There is a visitor centre, picnic and barbecue areas, toilets and a public boat ramp where boats up to four metres with motors up to 10 h.p. may be launched.

Also, private businesses operate a camping ground, kiosk, boat tours and helicopter scenic flights. The camping ground has ablution blocks and sites (with and without power) for tents, caravans and coaches. Groceries, film, souvenirs and petrol may be purchased on site.

Edith Falls

Edith Falls is 60 kilometres north of Katherine on a sealed road. It is one of the most popular tourist destinations in the region and is often included as part of Nitmiluk.

Below: *Edith Falls offer excellent swimming opportunities in beautiful surroundings.*

It consists of a stunning chain of falls cascading over cliffs to a deep and large pool of clear water where swimming is safe all year round. The Falls plummet over the western most area of the Arnhem Land escarpment and, during the Wet, they are among the most spectacular in the Top End.

Just before the main fall, a gurgling torrent, there is a small rockhole of crystalline and cool water nestled among boulders worn by time. It is one of the most charming and attractive water holes I have ever seen. There is a defined trail which gives the walker an alternative return trip via the southern side of the river.

Edith Falls is a perfect spot to relax and laze about watching the marvellous sunsets and having an occasional swim. There are modern ablution facilities, wood barbecues, a kiosk and excellent park information.

Katherine Low Level

You will find this delightful and easy to access 105 hectare nature park five kilometres south west of Katherine off the Victoria Highway. Basically the park is a recreational retreat consisting of manicured and well vegetated grounds on the banks of the Katherine River.

It is one of the town's most popular swimming spots. Bushwalkers have an opportunity to explore and observe the abundant natural attractions close to the town.

The fauna includes Black and Little Red Flying Foxes which have taken over trees along the river bank. If you are patient, you might be rewarded with the sight of the Northern Snapping Turtle which also lives here.

Fishing enthusiasts will find plenty of Barramundi and Black Bream (Sooty Grunter) in the waters of the park which are also ideal for canoeists.

Visitor facilities include pleasant, landscaped picnic grounds with barbecues, tables and toilets.

Be warned that the water level here can rise dramatically and currents can become strong following heavy downpours in the wet season.

Umbrawarra Gorge

About 100 kilometres north of Katherine is Pine Creek, the site of a gold rush more than 100 years ago. This was a mini-Ballarat where a handful of European and several thousand Chinese diggers flocked to seek their fortune. The elusive quality of history is very much alive here with relics of Chinese diggings in evidence everywhere.

Well worth visiting is the town's 'Miners Park' which houses historic mining equipment collected and carefully restored with funds from the National Trust's Bicentennial Project. There is also a museum and library, the old railway station, and a great hotel where, with some luck, you may share a drink with Crocodile Dundee frontier types. They are becoming a rarity in the Northern Territory but if you are going to meet them anywhere, this is probably the best place for encounters.

About 25 kilometres west of the Stuart Highway, just south of Pine Creek, is the 972 hectare Umbrawarra Gorge Nature Park. Consisting of an exceptionally beautiful and extensive gorge, the park has several swimming holes of dark water and some captivating sites with Aboriginal rock art.

There is history here as well, for Umbrawarra was a tin mining region from the 1870s onwards. Early this century some pretty rough characters, originally all Europeans, congregated here and from them emerged the first trade union in the Northern Territory, the Umbrawarra Tin Miners Association. The entire Labor movement in the Territory was born in this wilderness. I find it somewhat touching that great dreams of socialism were fiercely debated here, amidst the sardonic loneliness of the bush.

The Europeans and their dreams of collectivism departed after they failed to make a go of the tin deposits and an epidemic of malaria killed about

50 of them in 1910–11. They were replaced by about 150 very tough Chinese miners who persisted with the diggings until 1925 when, defeated by the country, they too went.

Wagaman Aboriginal people say that Umbrawarra marks the Dreaming track of Kuna-ngarrk-ngarrk, the White-bellied Sea-Eagle which caught and ate Barramundi at the entrance of the Gorge. The Wagaman believe that the quartz flakes embedded in the area's granite boulders are scales from the Barramundi and that the solid quartz outcrops are the eagle's droppings.

Umbrawarra supports colonies of the Short-eared Rock-wallaby and Rock Ringtail Possum. Bushwalkers may take this opportunity to rock-hop the entire five kilometres of the Gorge, but shorter walking tracks are also available.

There is an area designated for camping and the Parks and Wildlife Commission asks that you use the fireplaces as provided. Visit only in the dry season. During the wet season, the road is often cut by flooding at creeks after heavy rains making the Gorge inaccessible.

Douglas Hot Springs

Tjuwaliyn (Douglas Hot Springs) is a 3107 hectare nature park about 130 kilometres north west of Katherine. Access is via a well-signposted 20 kilometre gravel road off the Stuart Highway north of Hayes Creek. The road may be subject to wet season closures but is normally open all year round.

The park is owned by the Wagaman Aboriginal people and is managed by Parks and Wildlife Commission rangers.

As its name indicates, the park includes thermal springs which bubble up into the Douglas River forming a series of pools with striking sandbars. The river was named after the Territory's first civilian administrator Captain Bloomfield Douglas, quite a character.

Douglas Hot Springs contains several sacred sites of significance to its traditional Wagaman owners who use the area for hunting and for their ancient ceremonies. A word of warning; the springs are very hot. Before taking a dip, you would be well advised to test the springs with your big toe. I did and decided against a hot bath just then.

They are the result of volcanic activity under the ground although the water is rain water. The nearby escarpment acts as a catchment area for

Right: *Named after a tin mine which operated in the area before the First World War, Umbrawarra Gorge is a peaceful retreat rich in natural beauty and Aboriginal and European history.*

the rain which seeps to a depth of about 600 metres before being forced back to the surface through a fault line. If you do not fancy being boiled alive, there is a swimming hole of rare beauty nearby where you can paddle about in lusciously cool waters. The waters adjacent to the Hot Springs are considered safe although they are frequented by freshwater crocodiles.

The warm humid environment here has created a veritable oasis which attracts nocturnal animals including a vast colony of Flying Foxes, Bandicoots and Northern Quolls.

There are extensive bush camping, picnic and barbecue facilities, water and pit toilets.

Butterfly Gorge

You cannot leave this area without visiting the Butterfly Gorge Nature Park, about 17 kilometres from Hot Springs via a track over black soil plains recommended for four-wheel-drive vehicles only, although conventional vehicles can make it with care during the Dry. The track is inaccessible during the wet season.

A walk from the parking area to the Gorge itself takes you into a tangled and dark rainforest on the side of a murky creek. The sun may shine brightly overhead, but in the forest there are only dappled, flickering shadows. Freshwater crocodiles abound in the creek and they scamper into the water at the sight of approaching humans.

The ground is soft with the decaying remains of old foliage. Some of the paperbark trees are gigantic, up to 45 metres tall, kings in a kingdom that on occasions includes human beings weaving their way between mountainous trunks. The walk takes about half an hour. Butterfly Gorge is an exquisite little gorge which derives its name from the swarms of Common Crow Butterflies that sometimes gather here. The best observation point is a knoll on top.

The rock pools and the large pool at the base of the Gorge are excellent swimming spots free of saltwater crocodiles.

The Parks and Wildlife Commission advises that when walking to the gorge, watch your footing and take care not to dislodge loose rocks, especially when other visitors are below. Camping is prohibited at Butterfly Gorge, but the park is within easy reach of the Douglas Hot Springs campground, making for an excellent day trip.

*Left: Butterfly Gorge is named because swarms of butterflies sometimes gather there. **Below:** The Katherine region can claim to provide a home for the uncommon Orange Horseshoe Bat.*

Around Timber Creek

imber Creek, about 300 kilometres south west of Katherine, is the perfect place to launch your exploration of the Victoria River District which includes the world class national parks of Gregory and Keep River.

The Victoria River District, better known in the Territory as the VRD, is one of Australia's most famous pioneering pastoral regions and linked to significant families in Australian history such as the Duracks and Vesteys and, more recently, Holmes a Court who are the owners of the Territory's own 'Big Run'. There are also some significant connections here with the convergence of Aboriginal self-determination and the end of European frontier expansion.

The river itself, the region's centrepiece, was discovered by Lieutenant John Lort Stokes and Captain John Wickham in 1839, about 30 years before Port Darwin was established, and named after Queen Victoria.

The area was opened up for European settlement by explorer Augustus Charles Gregory whose 1855–56 expedition to northern Australia ranks among the most difficult undertakings in the annals of Australian explorations. Gregory led a party of 18 men, including an artist, Thomas Baines, botanists and a geologist. They had 50 horses, 200 sheep, and enough supplies for 18 months. It was therefore one of the best equipped expeditions to venture into the wilds of the north. They set sail for the Victoria River in the barque *Monarch* and schooner *Tom Tough* which arrived at Treachery Bay (later named Pearce Point) on 18 September 1855 to begin their incident-filled journey.

They were followed by missionaries, adventurers, prospectors and pastoralists. Conflict with some of the most warlike Aboriginal

people in Australia was inevitable and it shaped the blood soaked history of this region. As elsewhere, boomerangs and nulla-nullas were no match for Martini-Henri repeat rifles and the tribes, one by one, were subjugated or killed. They didn't go with a whimper. This land, like the rest of the Territory, was surrendered only after a ferocious struggle which lasted until relatively recently.

While you camp out near any one of the marvellous billabongs and rivers of this area, you may want to read *Hidden Stories* by Deborah Bird Rose, an exceedingly good account of the VRD's rich history. Ernestine Hill's *The Territory* gives a vivid account of the period. She does not mince words when she says:

'The business of establishing a cattle empire depended upon killing. To the new station you brought working blacks from some far country—no conspiracies, they were terrified of the 'bush niggers,' and for protection of your 'muckity,' musket, never ventured out of your sight. There was 'quiet nigger' country and 'bad nigger' country. . .'

As Bird Rose says, 'the Victoria River Valley was, from the point of view of the settlers, most assuredly, 'bad nigger' country.'

The cattle barons, tough and resourceful, established their empires and around them grew a whole industry of cattle duffers or poddy dodgers, who were in fact welcome by the cattlemen, mainly because the ruffians came at a price well worth paying. They were the buffer between the established cattle stations and the wild 'bush niggers'. The Aboriginal people had to go through them first before they could get to the established stations, and that was a hard task because these white men were a hard lot.

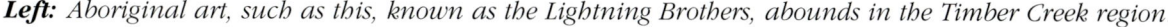

Left: Aboriginal art, such as this, known as the Lightning Brothers, abounds in the Timber Creek region.

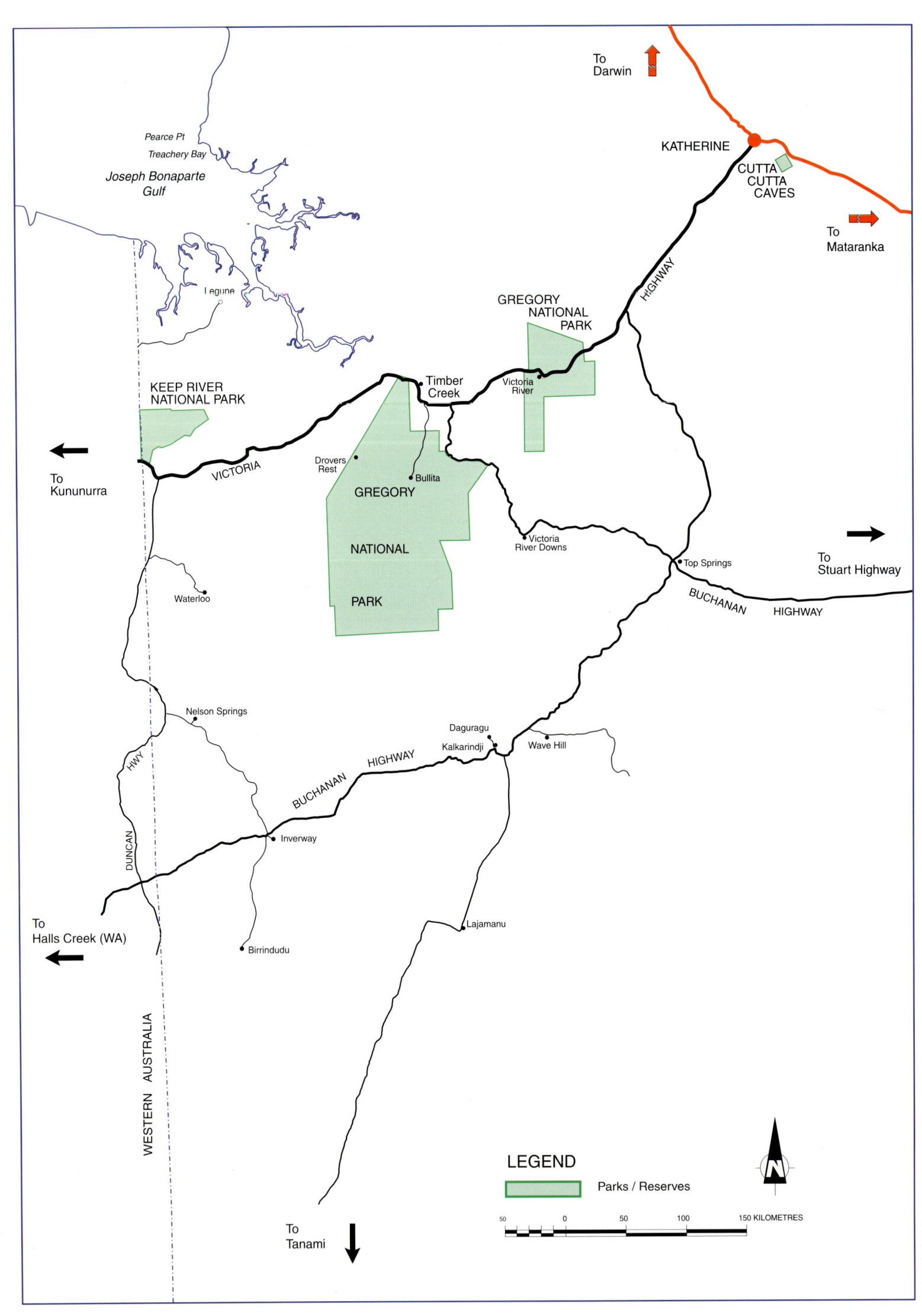

Typical of the ruffians was Brigalow Bill who took up a block on the west side of the Victoria River around 1908. His notorious career—certainly comparable to the best that the American Wild West had to offer—ended in 1910 when he was ambushed and killed by a group of Aborigines. But the killing was not always between blacks and whites. Early this century, great inter-tribal wars over women also took a dreadful toll on the Aboriginal population in VRD, as did smallpox epidemics.

In 1967, Aboriginal people here began a determined and long fight back which eventually led to a degree of self determination. In that year, a group of Gurindji stockmen led by Vince Lingiari went on strike for higher pay at Wave Hill. When the rise was not granted, they moved to nearby Wattie Creek to sit out the strike. This simple industrial dispute escalated into demands for land, first a small block of about seven square kilometres around Wattie Creek, then into land rights which were granted in 1976.

There are a number of ways to reach this fascinating area. The most comfortable has already been mentioned. It is via the Victoria Highway, a sealed road into Western Australia. But for those who feel a bit more adventurous and want to take in as much of the country as possible, you would be better advised to travel down the Buchanan Highway to a place called Kalkarindji, half way between Wave Hill on the north east and Daguragu on the south east. That is the heart of Gurindji country.

From Daguragu, drive straight north to Mt Sanford Station on a well graded and well-kept track. This is a showpiece manicured station reminiscent of South Australian or even Victorian pastoral properties, but as you cross the last gate before heading towards the Humbert River on the northern boundary, you move into another world.

The 40 kilometre stretch from the gate to the Humbert River Station in the north takes you into one of the most scenic parts of the Territory and hardly anyone visits it. The rough, strictly four-wheel-drive track winds among well forested hills and magnificent escarpments, criss-crossed by many waterways which are dry in the winter but flooded during the Wet and impassable.

About 25 kilometres from the gate is Wickham Gorge. This amazing gorge does not even feature in maps. There are thousands of other escarpments and creeks in the Top End, but what makes this one exceptional is that it includes an immensely dark primeval forest stretching for about 10 kilometres. Here is a jumbled mess of Northern Box, fine tall Eucalypt, Whitewood and Beefwood, with thick

Below: *Pandanus line the water of the Humbert River.*

Above: *The peaceful dry season waters of the Wickham River flow through a gorge in Gregory National Park.* **Below:** *The setting sun highlights Wickham River.*

vines hanging lazily to the clean ground mulched by millions of years of plant decay. It is an inviting forest, mysterious but welcoming. There is infinite peace here in this utterly remote corner which is waiting to be discovered. At some future stage it might be developed for use by bushwalkers and campers but right now it is almost unexplored and virgin.

Gregory National Park

At 12,872 square kilometres, Gregory National Park is the Territory's second largest after Kakadu. The park has two sections separated by the Aboriginal owned Stokes Range area.

The park's establishment came about as the result of the experiences in the Gregory area of a former well known Territory politican, Roger Steele. Mr Steele spent many years as a stockman in the area and married the daughter of a local legend, Charlie Schultz. Later, when he became a politician, he was instrumental in establishing the park which covers all of Bullita and former portions of Innesvale, Fitzroy, Auvergne, Delamere, Humbert River and Victoria River Downs stations, and it includes Gregory's Tree Historical Reserve—a total area of a staggering one million hectares, mostly undeveloped and untouched wilderness.

And there is a lot in it, from spectacular gorges and ranges to cool billabongs and forests. The rivers carry abundant fish and there are safe waterholes for swimming.

The park contains sites of great significance to local Aboriginal people. Members of the Wardaman, Ngariman, Ngaliwurri, Nungali, Jaminjung and Karrangpurra Aboriginal groups have had a long association with this land

Above: *Gregory's Tree, one of many historical Boabs in the region, is where Augustus Gregory carved his mark while exploring the area.* **Below:** *Aboriginal rock engravings are found in the Gregory National Park.*

Above: *A turtle lumbers its way into clear waters.* **Right:** *Boab trees, like these at Bullita, are unique to North West Australia.* **Overleaf:** *Victoria River flows through spectacular country near Gregory Creek Junction.*

reflected in substantial rock art. Indeed the diversity and richness of art sites here rivals any other known area in the Territory with the possible exception of Deaf Adder Gorge in Kakadu. Those include uncommon rock engravings; a type of hawk trap not known to exist elsewhere; rock shelters and occupational sites of great archaeological significance. Several sacred sites have been identified and registered.

The European history of this area began with John Wickham and John Lort Stokes. The explorer Augustus Gregory made his base camp at Gregory's Tree Historical Reserve. Gregory carved his name and dates on the tree, a magnificent Boab lording it over the Victoria River and now registered with the National Estate. Alexander Forrest's expedition traversed the Wickham River area in 1879.

The flora and fauna of this huge park reflect a geographical transition between tropical and semi-arid zones. The arid southern sections are characterised by spinifex covered hills. The northern portion is dissected by riverine flora. Remnants of ancient vegetation are found in the Victoria River sector with a curious Livistona species, the Victoria Palm performing an amazing balancing act on the red escarpments. The Boab is the region's most distinctive tree. The so-called 'Bottle Tree', found only in north west Australia,

was first described in this district by Ferdinand von Mueller in 1856.

Communities of the Northern Grey Box (*Eucalyptus argillacea*) occur only in Gregory National Park, and a species appropriately named *Acacia jasperensis* is found around the Park's Jasper Gorge.

A variety of native animals call Gregory Park home. Bird watchers may spot the tiny rare Purple-crowned Fairy Wren in stands of tall grass along the banks of the Victoria River. The Gouldian Finch, endangered in the wild and one of Australia's most beautiful native birds, joins other finches such as the Pictorella, Yellow-rumped and Chestnut-breasted Mannikin, Masked, Long-tailed, Zebra, Double-barred and Crimson. Lorikeets, Parrots and Cockatoos abound. The White-quilled Rock-pigeon can also be seen regularly, mainly in the semi-arid sector.

There are also fairly large colonies of Wallaroos and Agile Wallabies. And of course Saltwater and Freshwater Crocodiles are found almost everywhere. The salties are particularly active in the Victoria River which also contains healthy populations of Barramundi, Salmon, Black and Silver Bream and other fish species including the occasional manta ray and shark.

Four-wheel-drive enthusiasts have plenty of room to experiment. Access to Bullita Station from

Above: *Bullita Station Homestead resides in the region made famous by the Durack family.*

the Victoria Highway is by conventional vehicle but from there on it becomes rough and demanding four-wheel-drive country. Bullita offers a unique outback experience. You can sit under the verandah of the old homestead, a timber and corrugated iron building now in the process of restoration, and forget that the rest of the world exists. The river is about 20 metres down a slight slope, there are plenty of shady trees, including an ancient Boab with DURACK, the pioneering family's name, carved on it, abundant fishing, canoeing, or just reading and doing nothing at all. This place sheds the   20th century and enters another period, more peaceful, relaxed and satisfying.

The river carries a good body of permanent water with plenty of fish. No Saltwater Crocodiles are found here, so canoeing is safe although there is an abundance of Freshwater Crocodiles which can be seen from the top of the slope near the homestead. The ones near the homestead are cheeky little crocodiles accustomed to being fed by humans and therefore unafraid. I wouldn't swim here if I were you.

But just imagine camping in these surrounds with the smell of damper, roast beef, or barbecued spare ribs wafting up in the still air while wild cries of cockatoos and curlews play an awful cacophony as darkness takes over.

Below: *Wallaroos are found in reasonable numbers in the Victoria River District Parks.*

Above: *Keen and patient birdwatchers visiting Gregory National Park might be rewarded by sighting a rare western strain of the Purple-crowned Fairy Wren in cane grass along the Victoria River's banks.*

In the morning you can drive (only four-wheel-drive) to Limestone Gorge, about 13 kilometres away as the crow flies and give yourself a couple of days to explore these incredible formations and some marvellous rock art. Camp near Limestone Creek where it is safe to swim. The whole thing is sheer magic. The countryside is splendid and superbly scenic. You can lose yourself here which might be the whole idea in the first place.

If you are into four-wheel-driving, a feast awaits you in the bone jarring 92 kilometre track from Bullita especially developed by the Parks and Wildlife Commission. If venturing into the bush it is a good idea to fill in your destination in the books provided by Rangers at the start of all four-wheel-drive tracks. The run is divided into eight stops which can be done in a single day although that would be missing the fun. The temptations along the route are just irresistible.

Let me mention just three. The first takes you to Spring Creek Jump Up, an unusually beautiful series of water ponds among tall limestone hills and tower karsts. The water is limpid and inviting. It is an ideal spot for camping and recuperating from the gut-wrenching, eye-popping, teeth rattling journey to get there.

Nutwoods, and Boabs rest amidst other typical Top End shrubbery. Nutwoods in these parts are

Below: *Massive escarpments dwarf the aerial visitors.*

Above: *Victoria River District boasts remarkable landscapes.*

better known as Crocodile Trees for their rough textured, chequered or scaled bark, similar in appearance to the back of a crocodile. Some Pandanus fringe the clear pools below where the sunlight plays iridescent games. There is contentment in this place.

The second spot is about 21 kilometres from Bullita, at the junction of Spring Creek and East Baines (named by Gregory after his artist Thomas Baines). A very large Boab marks an old droving camp site. Boabs were traditional meeting places and camp sites during droving and mustering. One of the Boabs, with fine irony, was inscribed 'Oriental Hotel' suggesting it was a regular camp

with potatoes and onions. Tea, flour and sugar were just about the only other food carried which, occasionally, would have been supplemented by fish. Life around these parts has not changed that much and all you have to do to experience the past is to visit here.

The third camping spot is about 51 kilometres from Bullita homestead, at Drovers' Rest Campsite on the Barrabarrac Creek about 200 metres from the junction with East Baines River marking the convergence of the historic Auvergne Stock Route with the equally significant Bullita Stock Route. Here is pioneer Australia. The men who carved these stock routes in the wild didn't know it but they were writing themselves into the history books. Hard they might have been, but they harbinged civilisation. A few of their names, if not their thoughts, have survived in inscriptions on Boabs.

You can also fish for Barramundi to your heart's content. There is a three-kilometre long waterhole on the East Baines itself which can be reached through the Barrabarrac Creek. Below the campsite there is a natural boat ramp. There are only Freshwater Crocodiles in the waterhole, a welcome departure from the norm in the Victoria River where very large Saltwater Crocodiles abound. Bushwalkers can make their way from here to the escarpments of the north east where some mysterious craters with unusual and relict vegetation are found. Permits are required for overnight bushwalking and are available from the Timber Creek or Bullita Ranger Stations.

Good camping facilities are available at a number of sites throughout Gregory National Park. There is a major campground near Bullita Homestead and other camping sites are provided at Big Horse Creek, a splendid site with plenty of shade, toilets, water and barbecue pits, and at Sullivans Creek, east of the Victoria River Inn. The inn is a staging point for river cruises.

You will be taken in by Gregory National Park. It has a savage remoteness and a rare beauty which I find appealing. The best time of the year to visit this park is during the Dry, from May to the end of September, when mild sunny days and cool nights succeed one another with total predictability. During the Wet, day temperatures can soar well above 40°C. There are compensations for the discomfort. This place, like the rest of the Top End, comes alive after a few torrential rains and the sight of dozens of waterfalls and creeks in flood is unforgettable.

From Gregory you drive to Timber Creek, a picturesque township servicing the cattle industry in the area and, increasingly, tourism. The Timber Creek annual races in September are a classic Top End event attracting visitors from all over northern Australia. There are two hotels in the town with caravan and camping facilities.

site. Similar carvings indicating 'Club Hotel' and 'Royal Hotel' can be found along the Baines.

The drovers and their harsh existence come to life. A typical droving team consisted of five or six men—a head stockman, cook, horse tailer and three or so others. The camps were disbanded at first light. Food consisted almost entirely of beef

Left: *Palms grow in the valleys and cling to cliffs.* **Above:** *Keep River has a Martian-like landscape.* **Overleaf:** *Afternoon sun highlights the spinifex in the savannah lands.*

Keep River National Park

The 57,000 hectare Keep River National Park is 200 kilometres west of Timber Creek on the Victoria Highway. It offers great scenery, good camping facilities, bushwalking, Aboriginal art sites, birdlife and the most amazing geological features this side of the Bungle Bungles. Permits are required for bushwalking and are available from park Rangers.

The Parks and Wildlife Commission has established a network of walks. Deep into the park is the Jarrnam Walk, a name given to this entire area by the Mirriwung who are the traditional owners of the region. This walk is in my view the best. It takes you to the base of a huge escarpment where graceful palms grow in profusion. At the bottom of the escarpment, there is an inlet of sandy soil shaded by trees and ringed everywhere by grey rocky outcrops weathered by rain and wind. It is cool and inviting here, no matter how hot outside. Woollybutt Eucalypts, Emu-Apples, Turkey Bush, Gardenia, Banksias, Screw Palms, Acacias and Melaleucas are all present. Bushtucker, in the form of Green Plums and Billy-goat Plums (incredibly rich in Vitamin C), is abundant. This is a splendid gathering of flora. It is as if time has not moved. This place belongs more in the realm of fantasy than in the real world.

The walk meanders lazily to a rockhole gorged by erosive forces of water spouting fiercely over the fall in the Wet. There are fish in the rockhole: Sooty Grunter, Red-tailed Rainbow fish, Archers which hunt insects by jetting water at them, and Eel-tailed Catfish. Also, there are delicate blue water lillies that flower only during the late Wet and early Dry, paperbark trees with a few humming wasps, and luxuriant relict ferns growing on the surrounding walls even during the Dry.

I must say I was tempted to jump into the rockhole when I first visited this place a few years ago. I resisted the temptation mainly because it seemed a sacrilege to disturb anything in this corner of our lost Paradise. As it is, swimming in this specific rockhole is not permitted because it is too sensitive ecologically and therefore could be easily damaged.

The Jarrnam Walk is on flat ground and only takes an hour or so to complete, more if you want to savour something utterly exquisite. Without reservation, I will say that this is one of the most enchanting bushwalks I have ever taken.

Another short walk will lead you into a remarkable Aboriginal art gallery. Named the Nganalang Art Site it consists of a wide tunnel dug through the rock wall, according to Aboriginal Dreaming mythology, by an angry cockatoo which wanted to pass through to the other side. The

Above: *Keep River National Park protects a number of impressive Aboriginal art sites.*

Below: *Unusual rock outcrops are a feature of the Keep River area.*

more prosaic explanation is that aeons of wind and rain have managed to carve this almost perfect tunnel, an open cave offering shelter to local Aboriginal people. Over generations, they managed to weave an intricate web of rock art on the ceiling and walls which are beautifully preserved and well worth seeing. The Parks and Wildlife Commission has established an interpretive sign explaining the meaning behind the ancient art.

Finally, there is the Gurrandalng (Brolga) Walk that leads up a cliff wall and provides unequalled views of the park. The views are guaranteed to overwhelm your senses, take over your mind and throw your soul into confusion. Spread before your eyes is unimaginable chaos—sandstone escarpments, towering cliff walls, domes, turrets, ridges, crevices, gashes, terraces, ravines and thick woodland jumbled and tossed about as if by a capricious giant hand. The landscape could fit in several Kings Canyons. It dwarfs the spirit.

A Northern Territory geological team studied this interesting area in 1981. Their scientific report tells us what happened. The Keep River National Park contains parts of three major tectonic elements, namely the Halls Creek Mobile Zone, the Fitzmaurice Mobile Zone, and the Victoria Basin which formed on the Sturt Block.

What you see from the top of the Gurrandalng Walk is something entirely different. This

Above: *Uncommon in the wild, Gouldian Finches usually have black markings on their faces or, like this one, the less often seen red head.*

incredible landscape surely is the result of colossal and barely understood forces that shook the earth's crust millions of years ago in a titanic struggle to liberate the fire below. For some time, this land was beneath the sea and during this quieter period, when water dominated the scape, the sandstone and pudding stone that you see, similar to the Bungle Bungles to the west, were formed. They were then pushed to the surface by tremendous pressures. Having done the deed, the forces retreated leaving behind this piece of earth.

Local Aboriginal people have a better explanation. The custodians, Mirriwung and Gadjerong people, say that Gurrandalng was formed by two Aboriginal men who came from far away seas to the north. They collected grass and bushes, made a large nest and started to jump around making noises like the Brolga. As the country listened to all this, the two men changed into Brolgas, hence the name of the place and its appearance.

Later, much later, the chaos subsided and sanity returned bringing vegetation and animal life to this devastated but majestic land. White-trunked Eucalypts, native Gardenias, Ironwoods, Spinifex (this is still in the transition zone from semi-arid to tropical), Pindan Wattles and Silver-leafed Grevilleas are among many other types.

The fauna is also striking. There are White-quilled Rock-Pigeons, rare and endangered Gouldian Finches, Rock Wallabies and Sandstone Shrike-thrushes. Up until recently, Keep River was the only place in the Territory where the Splendid Tree Frog, *Litoria splendida,* was sighted. It has recently also been sighted in the Gregory area. A little goanna is also known only from around this area and in Western Australia. Colonies of the highly uncommon Ghost Bat and Orange Horseshoe Bat are also found in the park.

Facilities are very good. Keep River has two campgrounds, Gurrandalng in the heart of the park, and the more remote Jarrnam.

Rangers strongly recommend that walkers carry

Below: *A water monitor enjoys the sun on a rock beside its watery retreat.*

plenty of drinking water and wear sturdy footwear, hat and loose clothing. Walking the Keep River is most comfortable in the cooler months between May and September. A great park indeed.

Fitzmaurice River

The Fitzmaurice River is sandwiched between the mighty Victoria River in the south and the Daly River in the north. The Fitzmaurice and its catchment area, the Yambarran Ranges, are not a national park. They are part of the Bradshaw Station. But the region is so significant in Aboriginal, ecological and scenic values that it deserves mention in this book. Saltwater crocodiles have never been culled here and they escaped the indiscriminate shooting of the post-war years because access is difficult. As a result some crocodiles in the Fitzmaurice have grown to a monstrous size.

But the thing that most attracted me when a trip into the area was proposed back in 1990 was that it has hardly been explored. Much of the towering Yambarran Ranges remain virgin country. There are no records of anyone setting foot on the more inaccessible ridges and valleys. I wanted to know what was there. Accompanied by two Rangers, I entered this marvellous region

in September, at the end of the Dry. We took two four-wheel-drive vehicles and a 3.3-metre dinghy into the Koolendong Valley and reached the Fitzmaurice about half way between its mouth and headwaters, near a small but scenic gorge—the only one in the entire river's course. The valley is an elongated enclosure which stretches from Bradshaw across the river into Aboriginal land. It is old and broken sandstone country with imposing escarpments, fresh water creeks (some carrying permanent water) and a wide variety of flora and fauna. There are no tracks except those which have been carved by cattle. This is true wilderness.

We followed a rough north east bearing until all semblances of tracks petered off among a curious family of Salmon Gums near the eastern escarpment. You find beautiful Salmon Gums here and there at random, but I have not seen them grow in such profusion anywhere else. For some reason this family has found a home in a terrible and inhospitable place.

We made camp about 100 metres from the Fitzmaurice's sandy shore within view of a unique gorge. The water here is drinking quality at low tide. A four-metre crocodile lulled on the other side of the river watching the newcomers with some disdain. In the evening, we saw a rare

Below: *The Fitzmaurice River has cut this gorge through the landscape.* **Right:** *Typically beautiful scenery is seen at the region of Bullo River Gorge.*

Above: *The Fitzmaurice River winds its way through the surrounding landscape.*

spectacle as the setting sun painted the gorge purple and a myriad of birds greeted the coming of the night. This is a peaceful retreat where even the crackle of firewood blends with the forest and the water.

Both gorge walls contain some memorable rock art but I want to give particular mention to paintings found on top on the northern side. There is a hidden city at the top consisting of old sandstone domes and turrets which line up delicate natural walking paths of fine dust. This is a thickly forested area shading what seems a startlingly well kept European park. Flat-topped grey boulders have been strewn at random to provide visitors with comfortable seats. The whole thing is uncanny. No one has been here for a long time, perhaps hundreds of years. Yet here is this place carefully maintained as if its inhabitants

had just departed for holidays and expected to be back shortly.

Suddenly we came upon a very low cave with the most incredible rock art I have ever seen in my life. The numerous paintings certainly are very old and of such intricate texture that they could only have been the product of an ancient culture which probably experienced abundance. My mind might have been playing tricks. I sat stunned for a long time allowing the beauty around me to take over slowly. A gentle breeze rustled the slender boughs pregnant with dark greenery. A handful of scattered shafts of sunlight broke through to illuminate the scene and lend it an unreal atmosphere. There is deep and confusing serenity in this oasis. The layers of civilisation are peeled off one by one until nothing is left but utter and unrelenting tranquility. This is an unusual site.

The rock art is about a ceremony, maybe a celebration, and depicts tiny human beings linking hands. They are dancing or something similar and project well being. Their spirits, one is certain, still live among the rocks and in the trees and they seem to talk to the visitor. These are priceless paintings, the remnants of a fantastically old—maybe even kinder—civilisation which thrived here, on the high ground (useful for defence), but found plenty of food at the bottom. What happened to them or why they moved is not known. They left no traces. There is nothing like it around or indeed anywhere else in the Territory. The site has not been recorded or registered. I hope it will remain untouched.

Exploration of the river itself is interesting to say the least. A 3.3-metre dinghy is far too small to feel safe down-river because many of the Saltwater Crocodiles are bigger than the boat. Besides, the dinghy has to be pulled across several falls, not a particularly entertaining pastime with all those crocodiles watching. Up-river is cool freshwater and thick rainforest—wonderful bushwalking country. Fishing, as might be expected, is great everywhere.

And, on the way out through Claravale Station, you might want to pause and gaze at the imposing Yambarran Ranges. The landscape is something else. But it is the rock art at the top of Fitzmaurice Gorge that I shan't forget.

The Gulf Country

The Gulf Country of the Northern Territory is another of the Territory's great, unspoiled wilderness regions. It has remained pristine partly because access to most of it is not easy and partly because there has been little tourism infrastructural development.

The sealed Carpentaria Highway from Daly Waters, south of Katherine, will take you to Borroloola, on the McArthur River. It is not much to look at but the small township reeks of pioneer history. Here is where the ruffians moving from Queensland met the Northern Territory's arm of the law in 1885 with inconclusive results—the appearance of law and order was at least established, but the ruffians kept on coming. Cattle continued to change hands with astonishing ease and random killings were still fairly common at the turn of the century. Nevertheless, the glimmerings of civilisation were evident by the end of the 19th century. A police station was established in 1886 and the building is now in the national register. For some years, Borroloola, believe it or not, boasted one of the most extensive libraries in the whole of northern Australia until termites and mould slowly took their toll. The books that remained at Borroloola were relocated to various places during the Second World War and were lost.

Mt Isa Mines (MIM) operates one of the biggest lead/zinc/silver mines in the world in the McArthur River region. The deposits were discovered by adventurous prospectors in the early 1950s and appropriately named Here's Your Chance (HYC). But geographical remoteness and technical difficulties delayed their exploitation until the 1990s. Today, the mine is a substantial engineering and technological achievement which provides significant benefits to Aboriginal people at Borroloola.

The McArthur River Station is only 18 kilometres from Cape Crawford, the crossroad between the Carpentaria and the Tablelands Highways.

Some 60 kilometres before reaching Cape Crawford is Malapunyah Station, home of one of the Territory's leading pioneering families, the D'Arcy's. The original homestead, unfortunately, is in ruins but well worth a look. Behind the ruins is a marvellous tropical garden with a staggering profusion of plants and vegetation.

Shortly before reaching Borroloola, Caranbirini offers a scenic stopover. This waterhole supports numerous birds particularly at the end of the dry season and is a focal point for a wide variety of birds of prey prevalent in the area. In agreement with MIM, the Parks and Wildlife Commission manages the waterhole area as a Conservation Zone. Only a few hundred metres further on is a miniature "Lost City," a sandstone formation which although in scale cannot be compared with the Nathan River "City", nevertheless represents splendid viewing and is much more readily accessible.

Borroloola is rapidly becoming a fishing Mecca because the McArthur River is one of the most prolific Barramundi fisheries in the Territory.

There are reasonably good facilities to cater for the growing number of visitors, including motel and caravan accommodation. Fishing expeditions on the river itself and around the Sir Edward Pellew Group of islands, just off the coast, are offered by Borroloola tour operators.

The township also hosts the Lijakarda Festival, held in early July, one of the most important cultural gatherings of Aboriginal people in Australia. And for visitors who want a taste of the real thing, there is the Borroloola Rodeo and Campdraft which takes place in the second week of August.

Barranyi National Park

A visit to the Sir Edward Pellew archipelago is a must. One of the islands, North Island, is a 5421-hectare national park named Barranyi National Park, administered by the Parks and Wildlife Commission on

Left: Unusual formations can be found on North Island/Barranyi National Park.

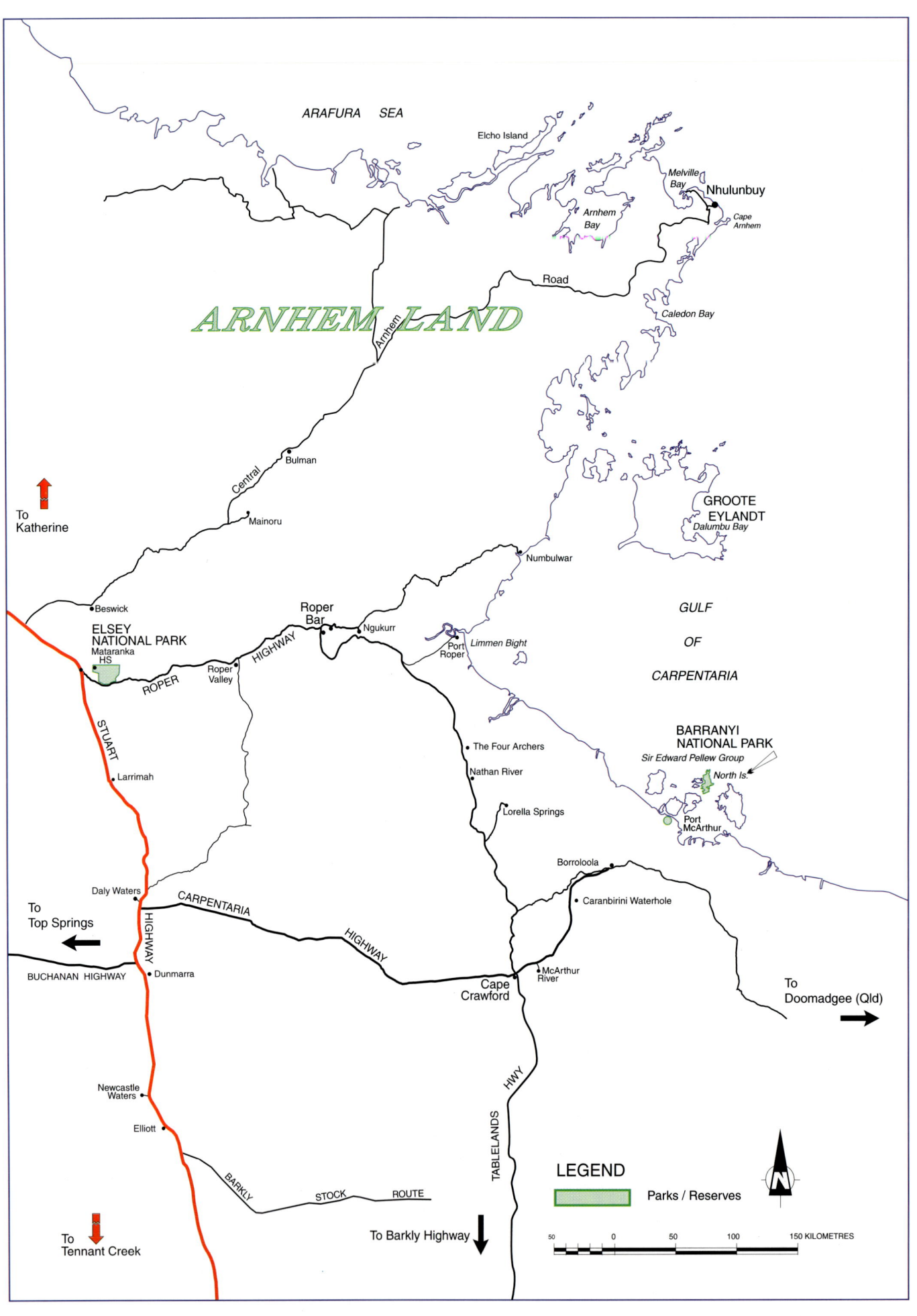

Above: *Sandy and rocky coastline are a feature of North Island in the Sir Edward Pellew Group of islands.*
Overleaf: *The mouth of the McArthur River sprawls to the sea.*

behalf of the Barranyi traditional owners who live mainly at Borroloola.

It is pleasurable to reach the island by boat from Borroloola down to the mouth of the McArthur River.

The trip down the river to the islands features a changing kaleidoscope of scenery including two rocky promontories standing guard over the river. They are Black Craggy and White Craggy on which the sun plays tricks making them change hues from deep purple shadows to creamy white, hence their names.

I once camped for the night on a strip of sandy beach fringed by scrub on Black Craggy. Old Man Johnston, a Barranyi from Borroloola, owns this little island and he told me stories over a wood fire while the huge moon rose over the sea and the fire slowly became embers. The stories, some of which cannot be repeated, are common among the Territory's Aboriginal people. They tell the story of Creation and a past populated by humans, plants and animals who spoke to each other and understood one another's language and lived mostly in harmony. The harmony may have been related to abundance. The seas are teeming with fish and there are plenty of animals on the islands. Food was never a problem for the indigenous people.

On the next day of my tour of the region, the choppy blue seas were alive with mackerel, literally seething with millions of fish on whom sea eagles, gulls and other predators swooped with glee. It was an astounding spectacle as our

boat threaded its way through the chain of splendid islands to the north.

Very soon we were at the aptly named Paradice Bay on North Island. This is a half-moon shaped beach of fine sand stretching for about two kilometres from a remarkably beautiful outcrop of limestone rocks in the north to a series of low sandy hillocks in the south. It nestles in the shade of casuarina thickets and monsoonal vine thickets.

The vine thickets are a rare and vulnerable plant community in the Gulf, probably crucial for the survival of some animal species which occur on the islands. So far, about 193 bird species have been recorded, as well as 42 species of reptiles of which five turtle species are on the endangered list.

Also, four of the 26 mammal species recorded in the Sir Edward Pellew Group of islands have not been seen on the Northern Territory mainland for some time, underlining the importance of conservation here.

These islands are beautiful and unspoilt remnants of times gone as well as important biological laboratories. And the fishing grounds are some of the most fertile in the north. All of which makes a visit worthwhile indeed.

Nathan River

Half way between Borroloola and Roper Bar in the north is the Nathan River Station, the home of an astonishing geological formation which extends

Above: *The Hidden City in the Nathan River region just towards the sky.* **Right:** *Caranbirini Waterhole is another cool oasis in the semi-arid landscape.*

some 15 kilometres like a vast megapolis of razor sharp ochre columns, Sphinx-like statues and arches creating a miracle known as the Hidden City. This awesome scenery consists of huge and graceful pillars effortlessly holding vast, perfectly rounded rocks, almost flawless cylindrical shapes jutting up high in the sky and big enough to allow a car through.

Beware, for it is said that a strange spirit lives in this maze of canyons and corridors. The spirit haunts this place and protects it. After Nathan's Hidden City, all else will seem petty. This is where the senses peak, the eyes, the mind, the words. They reach a plateau and ease off afterwards because nothing can be the same. To be sure, beauty, surprisingly fragile in this harsh land, is found in the most recondite corner of the Territory, but the combination of sheer and electrifying power and brutal grandeur that is the Hidden City cannot be found elsewhere.

After visiting this formation you return to the Station's homestead, set near a thermal pool of crystal clear waters against the backdrop of an imposing escarpment and a magnificent Pandanus jungle. This is probably the finest drinking water I have ever tasted. It is said to originate in the Star Mountains of Papua New Guinea and sifts under the Gulf of Carpentaria through an immense cavern or faultline. The theory is untested but interesting and may explain the quality of this water.

Nearby is the Limmen Bight River where the abundance of fish has brought about an explosion of saltwater crocodiles.

There are a couple of other magnificent attractions in this remote area. This is the home of the Four Archers, a significant rock formation. A little further across the Cox River, after a turn to the north and a short trip on a serviceable dirt road, you are rewarded with an awe inspiring encounter—a set of marvellous billabongs teeming with bird life and completely isolated from civilisation.

Finally, you reach Roper River, another favourite destination for fishing enthusiasts and for students

Below: *The Brush-tailed Rabbit-rat is an active climber and spends its day in tree hollows or the recesses of Pandanus leaves.*

of history. The German explorer, Ludwig Leichhardt named the Roper on 19 October 1845 on his expedition from Darling Downs to Port Essington.

He named it after one of his companions, John Roper who, in fact, had seen the river two days earlier on a scouting trip. Leichhardt wrote that the region was lush with plenty of grass, billabongs and wildlife of all kind. But he lost three horses crossing this wide waterway and was forced into a large detour before he could proceed towards the South and East Alligator rivers and towards Port Essington which he reached in December 1845. Leichhardt had planned an expedition of just six months. Instead, his remarkable journey of 4800 kilometres took more than 14 months.

Roper River Aboriginal people, particularly the Mara, fought fiercely against foreign invaders for

Below: *Unusual rock formations lie in the Abner Range, near Cape Crawford.*

decades before succumbing to firearms. Their story has not been told in any detail, but it is remarkable. What it says basically is that the Aboriginal people of this region put up a brave and desperate fight for about 30 or 40 years against Chinese and European prospectors, cattlemen, and police. The names of the indigenous war leaders have not been recorded for posterity. There were no set battles nor could there be. These people did not have the means or the numbers for foolhardy charges into the muzzles of Martini-Henri repeat rifles. Instead there were countless incidents and clashes. We do not know how many Aboriginal people were killed but it is a fair guess that a very large proportion of them died. All we know is that a state of continuous warfare existed here until well into the 20th century.

The site of several bloody ambushes on European and Chinese miners is at the appropriately named Hell's Gate. The graves that dot the landscape tell the story of the extraordinary struggle which could have only one outcome—defeat of the native inhabitants. A melancholy headstone at the old police station reads: "C.H. Johnson Speared by blacks June 1875." It was but one incident.

Perhaps the Aboriginal people took their dead to a sacred burial site nearby, where a striking rocky outcrop guards the entrance to a large cave. Three big monoliths, uncannily shaped like human heads, stand strategically, almost as if by design, in front of the cave's mouth. Inside there are plenty of human bones, the shins split and painted in various colours. This is also a major rock art site, unfortunately unrecorded and almost unvisited. Yet there is such an enormous historical and cultural treasure here.

This eerie and extraordinary region certainly is worth visiting. History may be a thing of museums elsewhere, but it is alive and well here in every tree and rock and every Dreaming story.

Let us now move to a completely different experience.

Gove Peninsula

About 54 kilometres north of Mataranka on the highway will take you to the Barunga turnoff for a trip of about 650 kilometres north east to Nhulunbuy on the Gove Peninsula. You need a permit from the Northern Land Council to travel this road into Arnhem Land which is owned by an Aboriginal Land Trust. The track is scenic, in parts marvellously so, but it is hard. If you want to save yourself a lot of time and some jarring you may want to catch a regular flight to Nhulunbuy from Darwin.

Whether you drive or fly, you end up at Nhulunbuy, the site of a huge bauxite mining operation by Nabalco. This is a mining town built in the 1970s. During the Second World War, an air squadron was based on the northern most tip of the peninsula.

A well known and well liked fighter pilot, William Gove, who was killed during a mission in New Guinea, gave the peninsula its name.

Missionaries established a presence in the area from the 1930's, a move prompted by reported attacks on Macassan trepangers in the area, the

Above: *A Brush-tailed Phascogale has hindfeet which can be rotated backwards enabling the animal to climb upwards or downwards with equal ease.*

killing of five Japanese at Caledon Bay in 1932, the murder of two itinerants shortly afterwards and the 1933 killing of a Police Office who was sent to investigate the Japanese murders. The Missionaries were destined to act as a buffer between the Aboriginal people and any non-Aboriginal visitors.

In the 1950's rich bauxite reserves were found on Gove Peninsula and the mining company of Nabalco began to build the town of Nhulunbuy, along with other infrastructure to support mining operations.

The traditional people opposed the mine and took their case to the Australian law courts. While their case was not won, and Nabalco was allowed to mine, the matter drew international attention and was an impetus for the Aboriginal Land Rights (Northern Territory) Act 1976 which gives

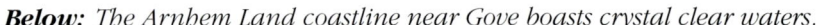

Below: *The Arnhem Land coastline near Gove boasts crystal clear waters.*

Aboriginal people title to reserves and the right to claim certain other lands.

These land mark occasions were sparked within an area of quintessential beauty. Nhulunbuy's beaches, arguably, are among the best in Australia and the town itself is in a picturesque setting.

About 11 kilometres south of the township is the airstrip. About 10 kilometres from the southern end of the strip there is a bush track, strictly for four-wheel-drive vehicles, which leads into a thick forest of Stringybarks and palms.

Then, quite suddenly, the first sand dunes appear and, beyond, a most spectacular shoreline. The turquoise sea is iridescent with tiny blue stars that dissolve with a soft murmur on the beach's snow-white powder. Only the breeze and the lazy surf break the chant of birds feeding on Casuarinas while terns skip out of the way.

Let me make a bold statement. I believe the stretch of coast between Cape Arnhem on North East Arnhem Land and Port Bradshaw further to the south, about 35 kilometres, is the most stunning shoreline on Earth.

Magnificent dunes are interspersed by limestone outcrops so weathered that they look like delicate oyster platters on top of one another.

At Cave Beach, a small cove where a stream runs into the sea, a clump of paperbark trees blends into the rocks and sand.

The experience is unforgettable. On the way back to Nhulunbuy, the track winds on the edge of a formidable Pandanus forest, an emerald jewel forbidden to any but the brave and resourceful as this land can be dangerous. Anyone without knowledge of the area and what it hides might become a victim of crocodiles and snakes which find a natural home in the large forest. From Blue-water Marlin to Mackerel, from Coral Trout to Cod, Trevally, Barracuda, Turrum and Barramundi, these waters teem with all kinds of fish. And the string of islands nearby provide idyllic surrounds for visiting fishermen. As access to the islands is restricted intended visitors must refer to the Northern Land Council for permits.

But just imagine yourself hooking Queenfish and retiring to an improbably beautiful cove fringed by forest to watch the sun go down with the delicious aroma of grilled fish wafting around you.

The weather is balmy all year round although storms and violent cyclones may lash the area periodically during the monsoons.

This is all Aboriginal land and a permit is required from the owners. Write to the Permits Officer, Bureau of the Northern Land Council at PO Box 820, Nhulunbuy for an application form. An additional permit is required to visit recreation areas including all beaches. These permits can be obtained from the Dhimurru Land Management Aboriginal Corporation.

These coastal people do not ask much. All they want is for visitors not to leave a mess behind.

Below: *Melville Bay on the Gove Peninsula is a quiet spectacular stretch of water.*

Around Darwin

Darwin is the perfect base to launch an exploration of the Northern Territory's Top End. There are about 16 easily accessed parks and reserves around Darwin, ranging from the World Heritage-listed area of Kakadu to Litchfield National Park, comprising the best that northern Australia has to offer.

The city is a fascinating destination in itself. It is Australia's only tropical capital city and the only one which has been razed by enemy bombing and by periodic cyclones. Darwin is a tough old survivor. It has emerged bigger and brighter after every disaster. Today, about 76,000 people call Darwin home and 25,000 more live in the satellite town of Palmerston, about 15 kilometres east south east, and in the surrounding rural area, the Litchfield Shire. They are a cosmopolitan lot. Some 52 ethnic and national groups live side by side helping make Darwin a tolerant and interesting society.

The area was first named Port Darwin by Lieutenant John Lort Stokes, commander of the Beagle, on 9 September 1839. Stokes wanted to pay tribute to an old friend, Charles Darwin, who had been a ship's companion on a previous voyage to South America. Darwin, who would publish his monumental *On the Origin of the Species* 20 years later, was not on board when Stokes named this obscure but beautiful mangrove-fringed harbour after him and it might have remained just a dot on the map without a concerted attempt to establish a forlorn extension of the state of South Australia in the north.

It took a long time. There was no European presence here until the 1860s when various expeditions were sent from South Australia, then in charge of the sprawling Territory, to survey a

site for a settlement in the north. In 1869, after several failed attempts, the South Australian Surveyor General, George Goyder, finally mapped out a town—fashioned along Adelaide's grid lines—which survives to this day in the city centre. The streets are all named after the original surveyors: Smith, Bennett, MacLachlan, Knuckey, Woods, McMinn and Mitchell.

The original settlement, named Palmerston, could have been abandoned because it had nothing going for it and there was no real reason for its existence except the desire to establish a presence in the north. But the construction of the Overland Telegraph Line from Port Augusta in 1870–72 saved Palmerston (always better known as Port Darwin) which became, in effect, an Overland Telegraph station with a small number of officials and police to service it. Gold was discovered during construction, triggering a minor rush which, in the late 1870s, attracted some 7000 Chinese and a handful of Europeans, but it failed to do for the Territory what it had done for New South Wales, Victoria and Western Australia. No permanent prosperity came of it. The climate was too harsh, the country unremittingly hostile, and there was never much gold to go around anyway.

By 1900, Port Darwin remained a ramshackle settlement, more Asian than European or even Aboriginal, perched on the edge of Australia facing the Arafura Sea and the teeming continent beyond. A vicious cyclone destroyed the collection of shacks that was Darwin in 1897 and the people began all over again. Rebuilding was not difficult because there was so little of it to do. In 1911, South Australia, clearly defeated by the task of administering its huge dependency, ceded control of the Northern Territory to the

Left: Carpentaria Palms are a familiar sight, towering over many landscapes in the Darwin area.

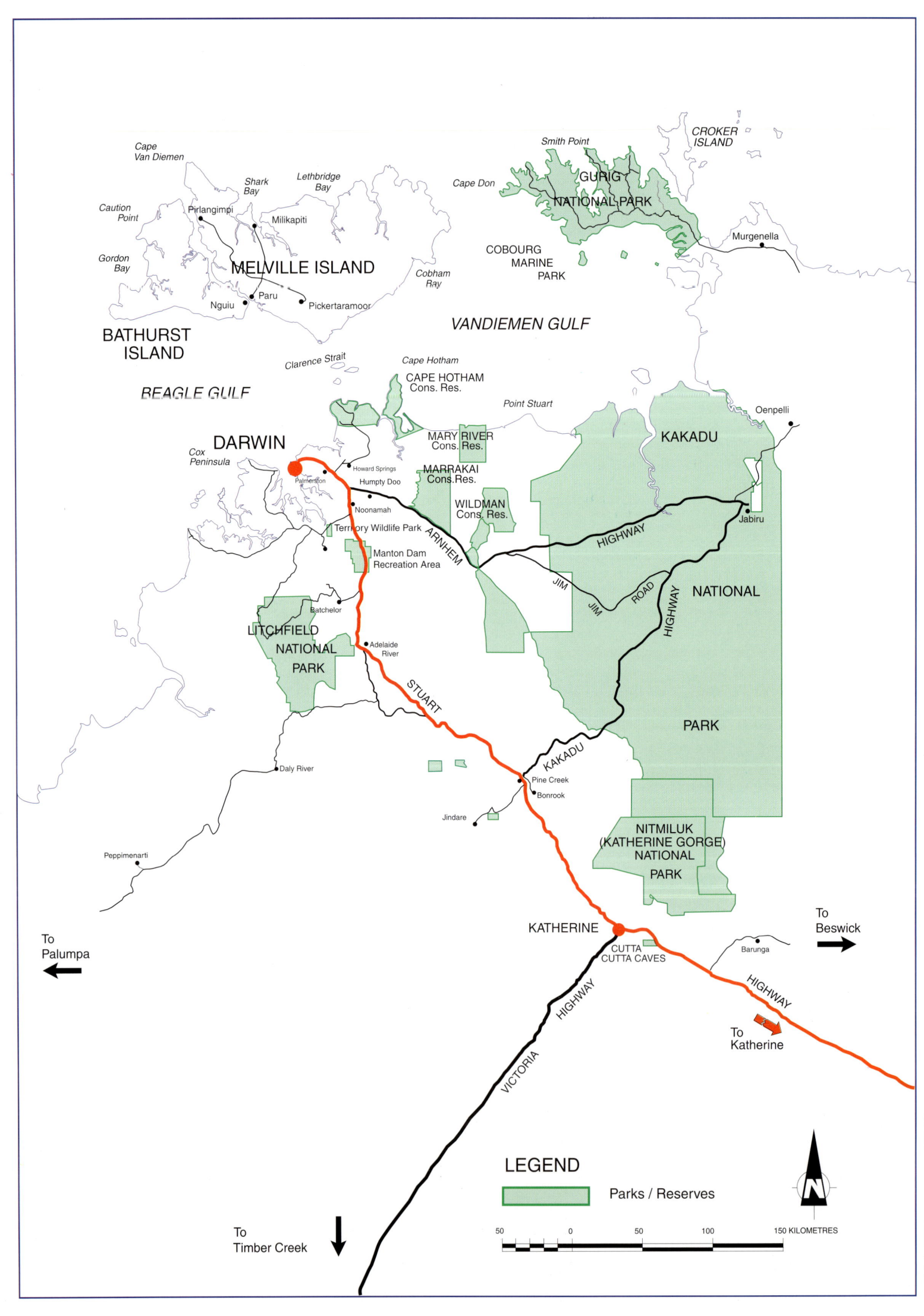

Commonwealth which found the job just as challenging and was ultimately just as unsuccessful as South Australia. About the only things of substance which had been achieved by 1911 were the Overland Telegraph and an incredible narrow-gauge rail line which stretched from Port Darwin south about 400 kilometres (eventually 500 kilometres to Larrimah). The railway embankments can still be seen from the Stuart Highway on the drive to Darwin.

Otherwise, with the exception of a handful of fine buildings such as the Administrator's Residence and the Commercial Bank (built in the late 19th century), Port Darwin remained a squalid backwater where almost every conceivable tropical disease, including malaria and dengue fever, was rampant and where the most elementary amenities were missing. "An iceberg of failure in a great sea of prosperity," was how one historian described Darwin at the turn of the century.

Things might have been expected to improve with the Commonwealth take over. Instead they went downhill. On 17 December 1918, a mob of about 1000 workers rioted in front of Government House demanding the removal of the Administrator, John Anderson Gilruth. This was the Territory's version of the Rum Rebellion and it was successful. The Commonwealth recalled Dr Gilruth in February 1919, after sending a gunboat to Darwin Harbour to ensure his protection.

In the 1930s, there was a military buildup, which brought more people to the north, but was woefully inadequate to defend Darwin and northern Australia from enemy attack. In 1939, there were about 5000 civilians in this remote outpost of Australian civilisation. That came to an end abruptly at 9.58 am on 19 February 1942 when a force of 188 Japanese planes launched a devastating attack from the same aircraft carriers that had attacked Pearl Harbour. Two hours later, 54 land-based Japanese planes attacked the RAAF aerodrome: 243 people were killed by the bombings and between 300 and 400 wounded. Also, 12 ships were sunk or put out of action in the harbour. Many houses were flattened and those left standing were vandalised and looted by Australian and American military personnel who believed the Japanese were about to land and did not want to leave anything of value to the invaders. The bombing of Darwin, followed by more than 60 bombings to the end of 1943, remains the worst wartime disaster on Australian soil. Today, a viewing platform and photographic exhibit near the Administrator's Residence illustrates the raid with chilling accuracy.

Tunnels were dug on the port cliff for oil storage, but were never used because by the time they were completed, the war had moved on, the Japanese had ceased to be a threat, and there was no need for them. One of the tunnels, below the viewing platform, has been transformed into a

Below: *Darwin's central business district creates a backdrop for an array of colourful yachts.*

museum with photographs and other memorabilia from the war years. Also, at East Point, there is a military museum with relics from those years.

Military reminders are dotted along the Stuart Highway all the way from Katherine. These were the airfields and army bases from which an all-out effort was made against the Japanese in the Indonesian archipelago, the soft underbelly of the Japanese conquests in 1942. The airfields were the launching pad for the longest bombing flights in the Second World War and the Northern Territory would have been the staging base for a final assault on Japan but for General Douglas MacArthur's decision to carry the main thrust of the Pacific war on an island-hopping campaign.

Darwin did not really recover from the war until well into the 1960s. By the 1970s, the town had become an administrative centre of some

Below: *Kakadu National Park is the home of the magnificent Twin Falls.*

importance and tourism was beginning to make an impact. Then, in the early hours of Christmas morning 1974, Cyclone Tracy struck and blew the old town away. Arguably, this was the most severe cyclone ever to hit an Australian city. Some 64 people were killed and several thousand injured; 30,000 residents out of a total of 43,000 were evacuated; 90 per cent of all housing was destroyed; there was no running water, sewerage or power. On Christmas Day 1974, Darwin had ceased to exist.

The city today is therefore brand new and very much the product of the years since self-government, grudgingly conceded by the Federal Government on 1 July 1978. Darwin's satellite town of Palmerston was only conceived in 1981–82 and construction started in 1982. Palpable prosperity and growth have been the hallmarks of Darwin for the past 15 years or so.

So there you have it. Darwin's often unsavoury past mixes comfortably with an exciting present. The future looks boundless but then, this has always been a city where almost anything is possible and indeed likely. The stuff of dreams is what keeps Darwin going—even when they come crashing down.

The city is Australia's best kept secret. Quite simply, you can have a good time here while you plan your exploration trips, starting with the best known national park in the Top End, Kakadu.

Kakadu National Park

A World Heritage listed area, Kakadu is a 19,000 square kilometre national park about 250 kilometres east of Darwin on the Arnhem Highway. This park is in a class of its own. It has been popularised by the movie 'Crocodile Dundee' although no film can really do it justice.

Kakadu is more than pretty pictures and beautiful scenery. This is a savage, brutal park which sprawls with utter finality over a huge region of wild billabongs, vast floodplains and hundreds of kilometres of escarpments. It is not a nice land. Large Saltwater Crocodiles are everywhere. The murky dark waters contain danger. The escarpment and its gnarled rock formations are the home of spirits. Gorges, holding foaming water, do not make visitors merely wonder, they are a source of great awe.

This entire park has been wrenched in fury from Mother Earth and flung against the crust where it rests—twisted and contorted. The beauty and the beast live here, and that is what makes Kakadu so intensely attractive.

This is of course a personal viewpoint. A more objective view would see Kakadu as an ancient sandstone plateau averaging 250–300 mctrcs elevation. This is the rightly famed Kakadu escarpment which winds from Murgenella in the north to Katherine Gorge in the south.

The escarpment and rugged features which it contains are the catchment area for the South Alligator, East Alligator, Katherine, Roper and Daly rivers. Monsoonal rains pour into the magnificent waterways of Kakadu cutting through sandstone and carving spectacular gorges. And the escarpment lords it over lowlands teeming with unbelievable flora and fauna. The black soil plains

Previous Pages: *Water cascades more than 200 metres over Jim Jim Falls in Kakadu National Park.* **Above:** *Bolts of lightning blaze through the sky behind Pandanus plants—a common sight during the Top End's wet season.* **Right:** *Part of the Arnhem Land landscape, Mount Brockman overlooks Ranger Uranium Mine near the town of Jabiru.*

of the floodlands are the home of lagoons full of waterlillies and fringed by majestic Pandanus, Paperbarks, wild Hibiscus, Gardenia and Grevillea. The Top End eucalypts and ancient cycads are everywhere as well, creating a riotous ambiance of colour and monotony, of variety and sameness.

Kakadu was once covered by tropical jungle. Little remains of it except in some hidden gorges and sheltered corners where palms grow providing welcome shade for mosses, ferns and, sometimes, delicate orchids.

The landscape is more than two billion years old, the product of massive sedimentation and weathering. It has survived countless greenhouses and ice ages and is still going strong. The immense lowlands are flooded during the Wet and millions of birds come here to nest and procreate. About 290 species have been identified.

The unique environment has also spawned more than 1600 species of plants, 60 mammals, 120 reptiles, 25 species of frogs and 55 species of fish. Many are rare and occur nowhere else.

The local traditional owners named it. Kakadu is another way of saying Gagadju, one of the main language groups in the area. No one knows how long Aboriginal people have inhabited this region. Some rock art reveals that they have been here for 40,000 years or longer. This is the oldest recorded continuous occupation of a region by human beings. Certainly the rock art at Kakadu is by far the most significant example of prehistoric art in the world. Ubirr Rock, easy driving from Jabiru, is probably the best known art site which, as a

complement, also offers unsurpassed views of the Magela floodplains. Another gallery at Hawk Dreaming, near Cannon Hill, has paintings older than Ubirr. Nourlangie Rock and Sawcut Gorge are also sites of splendid rock art.

The art seems to show that the indigenous hunter-gatherer population here—as in other parts of the Top End, notably Wildman River—came fairly close to a sedentary culture. Certainly the art is very well developed, much more so than in any other part of the world at the same period. They were using stone tools such as axes and grinding rocks. They had learned to mash grass seeds to make dough and had established advanced social rites which governed their lives from birth to death. Many of those rites remain and have been refined through the generations. For example, Aboriginal people have a more sensible way of measuring the Top End seasons than Europeans who tend to divide the year into Wet and Dry.

The Aboriginal annual cycle consists of at least six seasons: Gunumeleng is the build-up to the yearly monsoon when it is hot and oppressive. Gudjewg corresponds roughly to January although it can occur in December when violent thunderstorms and heavy rain are common, generating an explosion of animal and plant life. Bangerreng is when plants are fruiting and little magpie goose chicks run after their mother. Yegge is April when the first dry winds signal the time to begin bush burning. Wurgeng is winter when night temperatures fall to 17°C or even lower on occasions and corresponds to June and July.

Gurrung is the transition from the cold to the hot weather in the month of August. It is the time to hunt file snakes and long necked turtles.

All this makes Kakadu an absorbing region for archaelogists and anthropologists.

The park, like Uluru–Katatjuta National Park, is administered by the Australian Nature Conservation Agency (ANCA), not by the Parks and Wildlife Commission of the Northern Territory.

This enormous national park also contains the largest proven high-grade uranium deposits in the world. Ranger uranium mine, on a slice of excised land in the middle of Kakadu, has been operating since the early 1980s.

Kakadu therefore is much more than a park. It is a bruising, hurting ground where Aboriginal history and mythology, the Dreaming, has clashed with the bustling, aggressive values of Western industrial society. And it is all happening in a ferocious landscape.

Visitors prefer to come here during the cooler months of the Dry. But the park is at its best during the Wet. That is when Kakadu really comes alive. By the end of the Dry, some of the park's most spectacular waterfalls, Jim Jim and Twin Falls, generally do not carry water. The rock formations are still worth seeing, but the spouting, raging, foaming torrent of water that makes the falls such a wonderful sight is often missing.

Access to Jim Jim and Twin Falls is by a dirt track which often becomes impassable in the Wet and is closed. Most likely to have a substantial flow is UDP (Uranium Development Province) Falls, now renamed Gunlom (Waterfall Creek), well in the south of the main park area. Readers may be familiar with Gunlom from the movie 'Crocodile Dundee'. It provided an idyllic background for one of the more romantic scenes.

Gunlom can be reached via the Kakadu Highway which stretches from Jabiru to the gold mining town of Pine Creek. The road goes through Yellow Water, a beguiling waterway where crocodiles can be watched at leisure from the comfort of a large flat-bottomed boat as part of an excellent Aboriginal-owned tour.

Two other singularly beautiful sites, Goose Camp and Red Lily Lagoon, have been closed for some years but are now open through the services of an Aboriginal-owned tourist organisation.

ANCA has built the Bowali Visitor Centre and the Warradjan Aboriginal Cultural Centre at Cooinda. They are both worth a look although nothing can be compared to submerging yourself in nature. To allow plenty of time to do this, visitors can stay at one of several resorts and good camping grounds.

Below: *Aboriginal rock art abounds in Kakadu National Park.*

Above: *Saltwater Crocodiles have become one of the Top End's best known wildlife icons.*

Murgenella

The road to Ubirr goes deep into Arnhem Land and, some 250 kilometres further to the north, to Gurig National Park and Cobourg Marine Park. A permit will be needed from the Northern Land Council's office in Jabiru or in Darwin. Road access to Cobourg is only possible in the Dry season of May to October although it is accessible by air and sea all year round. As the road is rough in places, a four-wheel drive vehicle is required. Take enough petrol for the return journey and it is also a good idea to take a jerry-can of drinking water.

There is a limit on the number of vehicles which may use this road meaning that only a handful of people make it to the Cobourg Peninsula. This adds to the secluded quality of this beautiful stretch of coast between Cape Don and the narrow isthmus near Murgenella.

Certainly the difficulties of getting there are forgotten immediately after sighting the place. This is likely to be the highlight of a visit to the Northern Territory.

The track to Cobourg first goes to Murgenella, about 120 kilometres from the final destination. It would be a dreadful pity to miss Murgenella. The name itself is evocative. Let the syllables roll bringing with them the salty breeze of Mur and the exotic romance of Genella. That is Murgenella, bounded by the mangroves and swamps of the Mini-Mini River system in the south and wattle-covered 25,000 year-old sand dunes on the coast.

This is an impressive empty coastline, an amazing littoral of cliffs, little ravines, hidden coves, beaches and bays stretching as far as the eye can see. The seas are glass-clear, spotted by banks of oysters and grey-brown rocks. The forest that fringes most of the vast beach has not been burned for a generation and is at a stage preceding rainforest. And it is all preciously empty

Below: *Lotus birds, or Comb-crested Jacanas, not only build their nests on lillies but use them as stepping stones to hop across swamps.*

Above: *Lillies colour the Murgenella wetlands.* **Below:** *Possums find a home in the Top End bushland but are seldom seen during the day.*

of human beings or development of any kind. The word pristine reaches an art form here.

Fishing is splendid. Queenfish, Barracuda, Spanish Flag, Coral Trout, Turrum, Reef Cod and Mackerel are among the abundant fish which can be picked up at will here even by a rank amateur. Then you can adjourn almost anywhere in paradise to barbecue your catch and wash it down with a cold beer.

The sand and sea are just one aspect of this magical area. The Mini-Mini mangrove delta is a haven for mud crabs, Barramundi and other acquatic life. Literally, it is teeming with fish and birds rarely disturbed by the lazy purr of an outboard motor.

A little to the south of the delta are the wetlands, as good as any in the Top End and better than most. Following the eradication of buffaloes and a great number of feral pigs, rehabilitation of the wetlands is well advanced.

Murgenella is staggeringly beautiful and, perhaps better yet, it remains largely untouched. This is a land of contrast. There is the shoreline, virgin and wild. Then there are the mangroves, just waiting to be explored and fished. The rainforest, cool and beckoning. Finally, the floodplains, as calmly majestic as those of Kakadu or the Mary River. An exquisite discovery.

Above: *Murgenella has a fabulous white beach coastline.*

Cobourg Peninsula

Only 120 kilometres across the isthmus from Murgenella is Cobourg Peninsula on the western tip of Arnhem Land. This is a treasure trove of undiscovered riches. The peninsula includes Gurig National Park and Cobourg Marine Park together totalling an area of 450,000 hectares of true and unspoilt wilderness, a precious retreat containing very special Aboriginal, Macassan and European historical values as well as significant flora and fauna.

Below: *Stunning starfish are reflective of Cobourg's vast array of wildlife.*

The two parks are managed jointly by the traditional Aboriginal landowners and the Parks and Wildlife Commission through the Cobourg Peninsula Sanctuary and Marine Park Board which gives high priority to the protection of this beautiful stretch of North West Arnhem Land. There are stringent provisions to preserve the environment here. Only 15 vehicles are allowed into the park at any one time and prospective motoring visitors must book months ahead to avoid disappointment. Alternatively, visitors can fly from Darwin to the Seven Spirit Bay Wilderness Lodge, an exclusive and isolated destination accessible only by sea or air. Nestled in natural bush, the Lodge is flush against the waters of the delightful Coral Bay on the western shores of Port Essington.

Port Essington is the place where the burgeoning, aggressive, pushing, empire building 19th century Europeans were forced to concede defeat. The symbol of that defeat, the Waterloo of British expansion in northern Australia, is to be found in the stark remains of the short-lived Victoria Settlement which is on a clifftop overlooking Port Essington.

It is difficult to imagine a more idyllic setting. This is a tropical retreat, a place of wonder, a magnificent bay full of sharp contrasts of blue seas, white beaches and forest greenery. Amidst the spectacular grandeur, there they are; the smoke blackened ruins of Victoria Settlement standing intact in their bleak majesty. Visitors will marvel at the glorious idiocy of the settlers and

Above: *The eerie ruins of Victoria Settlement on Cobourg Peninsula tell a story of hardship among early European settlers.* ***Below:*** *Known for their elegant dancing, Brolgas are often seen at Cobourg.*

those who sent them there in 1838. They faced no extreme perils such as were common for other explorers and settlers. There was no dangerous foe to vanquish here and no feat of arms was necessary or demanded from them. The ostensible reason they were asked to establish a settlement at Port Essington was to stop the French or another European power from doing so. But a French ship did find them in 1839, took a long look at the place, shared a bottle of cognac and several of rancid Bordeaux wine with the officers, and sailed away never to return.

The settlers were defeated only by nature, but nature gives no clues for their demise, certainly not at first sight. The exquisite blue seas and forest-fringed white beaches, fleecy clouds scudding above tall eucalypts and palms, the murmur of the sea - none of those things seems hostile.

Neither were the local Aboriginal clans—Agalda, Mudjunbalmi, Bgaindjagar and Muran (all four go by the generic name of Gurig)—who had occupied the region for around 40,000 years. They had some experience with outsiders such as Macassan fishermen who sailed to northern Australia from what is now Ujung Pandang in Indonesia. The Macassans had been arriving, for years before the Europeans, in fleets of up to 60 traditional prahus to gather and process trepang (sea cucumber or beche de mer). They traded metal implements, tobacco and liquor in exchange for turtle shell and fish, and a handful of local Aboriginal people may have travelled to Macassar with them.

A few Macassan words have persisted to this day, such as balanda (white person), binatang (insect) and mutiyara (pearl shell). Macassan songs also found their way into the local Aboriginal language and ceremonies. Their influence can be seen in the design of Aboriginal dugout canoes. And exotic tamarind trees which they planted, as well as some of the wells they dug and vats for boiling trepang, remain at Gurig as lasting reminders of their sojourns with Cobourg Peninsula.

But the pale Europeans were not transient people like the Macassan. Obviously, they had come to stay although whatever Aboriginal people made of them is not known. Relations between the races got off to a bad start after a serious incident early in the piece when a senior constable at the settlement, Sergeant William Masland, and four armed Marines apprehended some Aboriginal people for stealing. They put the suspects on a boat to take them back to the settlement. One of the men and a boy jumped overboard in an attempt to escape. The boy was quickly recaptured but the man dived into the water and did not stop when called upon. After he came up for air, he was shot by Masland and killed.

But, by and large, the two groups stayed apart which was unfortunate for the Europeans because they were not equipped for this country and they might have profited from the knowledge of locals.

They chose a site without drinking water, an awful mistake. There is plenty of good quality potable water within a 10-kilometre radius of Victoria Settlement, but, defying logic or common sense, this is where they decided to stay and plant the flag. Their settlement was razed to the ground by a vicious cyclone in 1839, just one year after their arrival and ships were sunk and stores lost. They dug three wells, essentially underground storage tanks for monsoonal rains. They quarried the unyielding cliff face for lime and carved tonnes of rock into building blocks. There is no scarcity of bush tucker around—succulent Red Bush Apple, Milky Plum, Native Nutmeg and White Currant—but these English folk had no idea. They probably would have been more at home in the Russian steppes than here. A lot of them starved in the midst of abundance. They toiled day and night for 11 long years and as many as 80 died.

They buried their dead in a cemetery adjacent to the sole garden in swampy ground near the beach. One of the graves bears an inscription: In loving memory of Emma Lambrick and child, wife of Lieutenant Lambrick of Hobart.'

Their remains lie underground, the debris of colonial dreams and symbol of a nation's chosen universal destiny. One wonders if Mrs Lambrick gave the slightest thought to the glorious surroundings she was leaving behind as she died. It is a deeply melancholic experience visiting the forlorn ruins of the Victoria Settlement which was abandoned in 1849. Isolation and difficulty of access have combined to ensure their preservation. And they have retained a sense of authenticity that many less isolated historical sites in Australia have lost to some extent.

Below: *Serene waters surround a sand island in Cobourg's waters.* **Overleaf:** *Seven Spirit Bay Wilderness Lodge is hidden amongst the beauty of Coral Bay.*

The Gurig believe this land was born in a single act of creation. They have invested the rock formations practically along the entire coastline with great significance. Many of the rocks are sacred and secret, and dangerous. Others are associated with ancestral beings of the 'Dreaming.'

Port Essington itself is the site of Banibuladjang, the Greenback Turtle Dreaming Site. The belief is that turtles can be multiplied by rubbing two special rocks representing turtles. But great care must be taken with this fertility rite for if the rocks are rubbed too hard, a deadly cyclone may result.

Then there is 'gargul gunak', the dominant eucalypt vegetation of the peninsula which is good because it is a source of food and medicine. Others are bad: 'Bani Bunji', a patch of rainforest where 'Arragaladdi', an evil spirit, lives. There are also two hills with large banyan trees which normally are considered benign but, for some reason, not in this area where they are highly dangerous and capable of causing great physical harm.

Finally, there is Cape Don on the foremost western tip of the park. This is the site of a tall lighthouse built in 1916 along with three homes of historical and architectural value. The construction is impressive in that it shows a touching and courageous faith in the future. The lighthouse was built in this remote corner of Australia with material shipped from Melbourne at a time when the First World War raged in Europe and in the Middle East killing millions and extinguishing the lights of Western civilisation almost everywhere.

Cobourg Marine Park is an important habitat of the Dugong which feeds on seabed grasses. Dolphins are common and whales have been sighted in deeper

Below: *Sunsets at Coburg are often magnificent displays of colour, such as this one over Black Point.*

water off the Cobourg coast. Saltwater Crocodiles are found in billabongs, estuaries and coastal waters. From time to time, they sunbake on the beaches. These are protected waters which are breeding grounds of six marine turtle species, including the Green Turtle, Loggerhead, Hawksbill, Olive Ridley, Flatback and, rarely, the giant Leatherback.

The fauna of Gurig National Park boasts large populations of bats and kangaroos. The wallaby's major predator, the Dingo, is also here. The dense woodlands provide a protective home to the Antilopine Wallaroo, Fawn Antechinus, Northern Brushtail Possum, Northern Brown Bandicoot and Echidna. More than 200 species of birds have been recorded.

The flora is equally exciting. Lush monsoon rainforest with extensive stands of palms grow near permanent water. Paperbarks, freshwater mangroves and Pandanus are common. The distinctive Kentia Palm reaching high in the sky can be seen among Stringybarks and Woollybutts.

And, if you are interested in geology, there is a fascinating story here. The landscape here was probably shaped by the drowning of river valleys caused by a rise in sea level following the latest greenhouse effect a few thousand years ago. Port Essington, for example, is the remnant of a river valley. And orange-red rocks at Danger Point and Smith Point indicate the presence of bauxite.

Other than Seven Spirit Bay Wilderness Lodge, visitor facilities include four self contained cabins at Smith Point and two campgrounds. Campers have access to barbecues, tables, showers and toilets. Local rangers have set up a series of recycling bins and encourage campers to use them effectively.

Left: Built in 1916 to warn sea-goers of reefs, Cape Don lighthouse huddles among some of Cobourg's woodlands. Above: On a high point over-looking the Adelaide River floodplains, the Window on the Wetlands Visitor Centre offers delightful views especially at sunset and sunrise.

An excellent cultural centre within the Black Point Ranger Station features displays on Cobourg Peninsula's Aboriginal culture, Macassan influence and history of Victoria Settlement, as well as extensive information on the area's natural attractions.

Fishing is what most visitors come here for and they are seldom disappointed. Dinghies can be launched at a ramp next to a pier at Black Point. Swimming is not recommended. These waters seem extremely inviting, but there are also potentially deadly Saltwater Crocodiles, sharks and Box Jellyfish.

Mary River Wetlands

On the way back to Darwin via the Arnhem Highway travellers will pass through the Mary River Wetlands. I call them the Mary River Wetlands to make the task of description simpler. But the large area to the south east of Darwin on the Arnhem Highway really is a continuum of reserves, parks, and a proposed national park which will rival Kakadu. This is a showpiece landscape which includes the extensive wetlands of the Mary and Adelaide Rivers. And, despite its proximity to Darwin, it remains relatively untamed and unvisited.

You can catch panoramic views of the area from the new 'Window on the Wetlands' Visitor Centre located on Beatrice Hill adjacent to the Arnhem Highway. The Centre, which is visible from the highway many kilometres away, provides an informative insight into this valuable area.

The Mary River is a series of billabongs and lagoons which are linked during the wet season to flood the surrounding vast plains and provide an environment for waterfowl of all kinds. This is where the yearly monsoon comes to rest. It is fairly tired by the time it gets here because it has travelled all the way from the Ganges Delta, soaked Malaysia and saturated Indonesia. But still, huge dark clouds approach the area lazily preceded by thunder and lightning, which make an amazing display, before discharging titanic amounts of water in these wetlands.

The water flushes out all the flotsam of the Dry and gives life to Barramundi and other fish. Estuarine crocodiles, stranded in the same billabong for months, are now free to travel although few actually move. Magpie Geese squawk contentedly. The rain is here. All the Mary River's channels and lagoons are replenished and, nearby, the mysterious and ancient Wildman rainforest, which has survived intact for many thousands of years, gets yet another reprieve. The striking granite outcrops of Mount Bundey, the river's sentinels, are an impressive sight silhouetted by lightning against a leaden sky. Brooding and old, they provide an impressive backdrop. So too do the waterlillies at Couzens Lookout.

Among other attractions, the Mary River wetlands include the Wildman Reserve, Delta Block, Mary River Crossing Conservation Reserve, Point Stuart Reserve, Shady Camp, Stuart's Tree Historical Reserve, Swim Creek, the McKinlay River Block and Fogg Dam, Marrakai, Harrison Dam, Lambells Lagoon and a variety of attractions on the Adelaide River.

There is great history here. Swim Creek and Shady Camp were named by John McDouall Stuart at the end of his epic walk from south to north. Swim Creek is so named because Stuart is supposed to have taken a swim here to shake off the stifling heat of the coastal plains. He took a risk with the Saltwater Crocodiles which are everywhere. He named Shady Camp for the generous shade offered by trees that have long vanished, grazed out by buffalo. Only a few scrawny fig trees remain although rehabilitation of this site is well advanced.

The buffaloes were shot out in the 1980s through the implementation of the Brucellosis and Tuberculosis Eradication Campaign (BTEC). With them disappeared a legend of the Top End—the buffalo shooters whose names can be found in landmarks stretching from here to Arnhem Land. The Hardys, Coopers, Cahills and Coles—truly rugged individuals who pioneered this land on horseback long before anyone thought of building a road all the way from Port Darwin.

The flora and fauna are typical of the floodplains. Tall grasses and sedges, tropical woodland, monsoon rainforests and plenty of paperbark swamps supporting huge numbers of mammals, including Agile Wallabies, Antilopine Wallaroos, native rats, Bandicoots, possums and Sugar Gliders. There are also Red-cheeked Dunnarts, Black and Little Red Flying Foxes and numerous species of bats. A tiny marsupial, the Common Planigale, which is usually no more than 10 centimetres in body length, lives in these woodlands. Dingoes are common and so are wild pigs.

As might be expected, hundreds of bird species have been recorded and reptiles abound—saltwater crocodiles and many types of snakes, including the deadly king brown and black whip. Fogg Dam houses a concentrated collection of water pythons and their prey, Dusky Rats. This concentration of wildlife gives Fogg Dam the highest recorded biomass of any area in the world.

Special note should be made of the Magpie Geese which were once common throughout northern Australia. Now the Top End wetlands are one of the species refuges and the Mary River wetlands are a breeding and rearing area.

Eucalypts dominate the flora although you will find plenty of Turkey Bush, Fern-leaved Grevillea (which tiny birds love because of its sweet flower) and common Fan Palms. The extensive floodplain system is fringed by natural springs which support dense stands of monsoon forest where you will find Wild Nutmeg, Banyan, Cluster Figs and Carpentaria Palms as well as Leichhardt Pines and freshwater mangroves.

Above: *The waterlogged wetlands create a mosaic scene.*

These coastal plains were formed at the end of the last Ice Age, maybe 6-8,000 years ago, when rising sea levels drowned river mouths and coastal river valleys. Very old and relic sand dunes (cheniers) at Point Stuart and north of Lake Finniss prevented saltwater intrusion of the freshwater wetlands. But in some areas dunes were broken down by either buffalo or, it is believed, blasted by fishermen to allow boat access to the sea.

Saltwater has penetrated deep inland killing thousands of hectares of paperbarks. Designed to stop saltwater from penetrating further, an artificial causeway barrage was built in 1987 at Shady Camp where fresh and saltwater flows on the Mary River meet.

Downstream from the causeway, Sampan Creek is one of the two tidal channels that help drain the Mary River system into the sea.

161

Above: *A Magpie Goose is commonly seen in the Top End's wetlands.* **Right:** *The Mary River system is popular with fishermen in search of a prized catch of Barramundi.*

This casual meeting of fresh and saltwater produces some of the most memorable Barramundi fishing in northern Australia. Here, the mullet converge to feed on algae washed down by a rushing stream of fresh water at the end of the Wet. Greedy Barramundi and other larger fish follow to feed on mullet. Saltwater Crocodiles, of course, think this is great. They are here in numbers to feed on Barramundi and can be seen on the river banks staring impassively at the fishing boats. Photographers who wish to add crocodiles in the wild to their record should come here or adjourn to a great waterhole nearby, Mistake Creek Billabong, with excellent wet season waterfowl observation vantage points.

Mistake Creek is on the way to Point Stuart, some 40 kilometres to the north on a dirt track which becomes impassable during the Wet. When you arrive at Point Stuart you will be standing on the precise spot that John McDouall Stuart stood at the end of his journey across Australia in 1862, his sixth expedition.

Stuart, a man with a well developed taste for strong liquor, is said to have drunk the alcohol in his compass on the edge of the ocean but the story is apocryphal and may not be true. Without doubt, however, he would have let the vast waters in front of his eyes wash away years of harsh struggle. He had succeeded where Burke and Wills had failed tragically, their bones bleached by the relentless desert sun. Stuart probably stood on

this mangrove fringed beach littered with clean debris and allowed himself a few moments of exultant reflection. He knew he had walked into the pages of history.

By the time he returned to Adelaide he was little more than a walking skeleton and died not long afterwards. His achievement mapped the way for the Overland Telegraph and, eventually, the Stuart Highway, so aptly named after him.

Little has changed since Stuart stepped into this hidden corner of the northern shores. The rough white sands are speckled by a myriad of tiny shells. Also scattered around are the twisted remains of dead trees which have been brought to land by angry seas. Due to the isolation of the area, apart from the ravages of a few passing cyclones, the land remains just as it was.

Back up the track to Shady Camp and then to nearby Wildman Reserve. This reserve will come as a complete surprise to you because it is such a delightful park adjacent to Kakadu, readily accessible by conventional vehicle, and offering almost unlimited options.

Near Wildman Wilderness Lodge is Wildman Lagoon, a stretch of clear water hemmed by blankets of blue, red and white lillies. The names sound pedestrian and do not do justice to this riotous beauty where little birds, Jacanas, hop gracefully from lily to lily and where crocodiles swim lazily, adding to the rare splendour.

I recommend Couzens Lookout for an extraordinary sight. During the Wet season,

literally as far as the eye can see, there is an expanse of dark-blue water festooned by gently bobbing lilies. Beyond are the flatlands of the Mary River basin broken only by clumps of paperbark forests. Immediately ahead is a crop of brown rocks jutting into the huge lagoon. In between are water and flowers. Above is the blue sky.

A short walking distance from Couzens Lookout is another sightseeing platform, North Rockhole which consists of a large pile of granite slabs protruding into the water. Nature's arrangement has fashioned it into a perfect jetty, a vantage point to soak up the marvellous sight and, with some luck, contemplate the antics of the odd crocodile sunbaking or chasing food.

This is also a site of significance for Aboriginal people who, in times long past, used the rock to crush nardoo or grass seeds for paste, one of the few sedentary habits picked up by these otherwise nomadic hunter–gatherers. The worn cavities in the rocks are clearly visible indicating a culture in transition, much like their kith and kin in Kakadu and identical to the natural development of all other nomadic cultures around the world through history. Almost certainly one of the principal reasons Aboriginal people chose this area was the abundance of fish in the lagoon. They learned to live with saltwater crocodiles which also abound here.

From the lagoon it is only a short drive across some floodplains (now recovering from the depredations by buffaloes) to a magnificent rainforest, a hideaway replete with the sounds and sights of the tropical jungle and cool even under the broiling midday sun.

The forest, named Brian Creek Monsoon Forest, is easily accessible and situated only a couple of kilometres from Point Stuart Road. It is a perfect place to relax, have a picnic or take a long walk through a landscape once common throughout northern Australia but now reduced to relatively small pockets like this one.

On the way to Darwin there is another reserve, the 1560-hectare Fogg Dam Conservation Reserve, which offers abundant native birdlife, extensive rainforest and paperbark stands, and excellent walking trails, including a viewing platform (with wheelchair access) over the Adelaide River floodplains.

Here you can see the graceful Brolga, the beautiful Black-necked Stork or Jabiru, White-bellied Sea Eagle, Kingfishers, many native ducks, herons, ibis and more. The adjacent rainforest is home to the Rainbow Pitta and the Orange-footed Scrub Fowl. And, as aforementioned, an estimated 6000 Water Pythons live in the area eating Dusky Rats which live in the cracks of the floodplain clay soils during the Dry. The relationship between Fogg Dam's Water Pythons and Dusky Rats—whose population here rates at an incredible one tonne per hectare—was the focus of an intensive study by Swedish wildlife scientist Dr Thomas Madsen.

Below: *An introduced animal, Water Buffalos have impacted on the the region's history.*

Above: *A white-bellied Sea-Eagle tends to her young in a huge nest of sticks.*

The study revealed a picture of near-perfect links in the area's food chain.

There is a 3.6-kilometre walking track with boardwalks across wet areas providing year round access for all visitors, including wheelchair users. The track begins near the carpark and meanders through a series of typical Top End habitats. It includes a lookout with spectacular views. Just one word of warning: there is no shortage of mosquitoes along the way, so come prepared with insect repellent and bring drinking water.

Worthy of mention are two hunting reserves near Fogg Dam. The first is Harrison Dam Hunting Reserve just a few kilometres away on the western edge of the Adelaide River floodplains. This reserve has been set aside for hunting wild pigs and waterfowl during the official open season and is particularly popular with bow hunters.

The other is the Marrakai Hunting Reserve, a multiple use area where hunters can shoot waterfowl, wild pigs or any feral buffalo remaining in the area.

Fire arm regulations in the Territory are strict. Shooters intending to use the hunting reserves must obtain a permit from the Parks and Wildlife Commission and must have this permit with them at all times.

This whole area is well catered with motel accommodation, camping grounds, toilets, showers, barbecues, and boat ramps. The Mary River Crossing adjacent to the Arnhem Highway about three kilometres west of the Bark Hut Inn is

Below: *The Black-necked Stork or Jabiru can be seen strutting along the banks of many Top End waterways.*

Above: *Monsoon forests like this one are dotted throughout the Top End.* **Right:** *Beautiful Florence Falls cascades into a pool of invitingly cool water in Litchfield National Park.*

a popular recreation area offering visitors picnic facilities, pit toilets and a boat ramp for convenient access to the Mary River. Camping is not permitted here but there are excellent camping grounds at Bark Hut Inn.

Take note of the crocodile warning signs. Visitors must exercise extreme caution and common sense at all times around here. It is foolhardy to clean fish or discard fish carcases along the water's edge, or to set up camp too close to the bank. Remember, Saltwater Crocodiles are remarkably fast animals on land. Crocodiles harassed at close range by photographers are likely to become aggressive. A telephoto camera lens is a far less risky means of obtaining a good crocodile photograph.

From the Arnhem Highway back to the Stuart Highway, it is only a short drive south from the road junction to Litchfield National Park.

Litchfield National Park

Litchfield National Park is the most visited national park near Darwin with upwards of 250,000 people each year. The 143,000-hectare park is 120 kilometres south of Darwin via the township of Batchelor or via Cox Peninsula Road and is about two hours easy drive from the city on the sealed road via Batchelor or a 46-kilometre gravel road via Cox Peninsula. When you arrive, you will find there is something for everyone; great swimming in crystal clear waters, bushwalking, some difficult tracks especially developed for four-wheel-drive enthusiasts, a spectacular plateau, woodland, magnificent scenery and excellent camping grounds. This is a park for the whole family to relax near large pools formed by cascading waters, take photographs or walk through rugged bushland.

The road from Batchelor, a historic township about 90 kilometres south of Darwin, provides a scenic drive to the Termite Mounds, Buley Rockhole, Florence Falls, Tolmer Falls and on to Wangi Falls. Wangi is a favourite for many visitors out for a weekend of lazying around and doing nothing at all under the shade. It features a large natural pool created by a tall waterfall which cascades gracefully from red cliffs. The entry to the plunge pool is fringed by trees and fresh lawns. The pool, a fairly large lagoon in fact, is bound by rainforest with tall thin Carpentaria Palms prominent as they search for the sun above the canopy.

A late evening or night swim to the walled end of the pool can be a marvellous experience. Only the stars, unbelievably bright and close in the

tropical sky, and the gossamer pale stream of water falling from way up, are visible. The rest is impenetrably dark and you can conjure up all sorts of tricks. Here there is only yourself and the night broken by shafts of translucent silver. Beyond is stygian night. In between are the odd bird cries and the occasional gust of breeze against the luxuriant primeval frond.

Then a slow swim back and a walk to the camp for the smell of burning firewood and a sizzling steak on a hot plate. Wonderful. Just make sure you have a mosquito net or some other kind of protection against insects.

In addition to swimming, Wangi also offers an excellent walking trail which leads from one side of the pool to the other via the top of the falls. This walk has won national awards for its design concept and includes a boardwalk, suitable for wheelchair access, carefully constructed steps, and platforms to give visitors the best opportunity to see superb panoramic view.

By all means, enjoy Wangi and its twin, Florence Falls. But if you want a truly unforgettable experience, mix your visit to those two sites with a number of other options.

Buley Rockhole, a series of cascading plunge pools, is everyone's delight. A walking trail from Buley Rockhole follows Florence Creek to the top of the escarpment and from a lookout point along the trail, a large stand of the Cypress Pine (*Callitris intratropica*) can be seen.

Nearby, Florence Falls also offers ideal swimming opportunities in a crystal clear pool at the base of the falls. This scene is a beautiful sight from a specially constructed lookout. Once again, this area also includes a walking track through the rainforest fringing the pools.

Florence Falls is accessible via a sealed road or, for the more adventurous equipped with a four-wheel-drive vehicle, an alternative track is available.

Another attraction is Tolmer Falls followed by the Lost City. As well, you might try to sandwich Tjaynera Falls (Sandy Creek Falls) nestled among some of the most remarkable flora in the park.

Tolmer Falls can be seen from a specially constructed lookout easily accessible from Litchfield Park's main road.

Set in a magnificent amphitheatre of imposing red cliffs, the Falls feature caves where hundreds of bats make their home. These bats represent important colonies of the vulnerable Orange Horseshoe Bat and Ghost Bat. To help protect these colonies, access to the falls pool and gorge is closed.

Below: *One of the most popular attractions in Litchfield National Park, Wangi Falls offers an inviting area for swimming, bushwalking and camping.*

Above: *Resembling a graveyard, these natural structures have been built in near perfect alignment by the termites living within.*

The Lost City is accessible via a four-wheel-drive track. The City is a natural formation, despite the perfectly shaped walls, narrow passages, huge gates and massive domes which are of such consummate workmanship that it is hard to believe there was no human intervention in their building.

From here you can test your four-wheel-driving skills on the track to Blyth Homestead and only a short distance south of the Lost City is another marvellous place—Tjaynera Falls. This plunge pool is accessible by four-wheel-drive vehicles to the camping and parking area and then via a 1.7-kilometre walk. The escarpment contains many delightful cascades and waterfalls and, associated with these perennially wet areas, small pockets of the same rainforest which once covered the entire Top End.

Before the eastern edge of the climb onto the park's dominant feature, the Tabletop Range, the road runs into an area that looks like a graveyard but is in fact one of the Top End's best collections of magnetic termite mounds. Each of these remarkable structures is orientated in a north-south direction so as to present the eastern and western faces of the mounds to the morning and afternoon sun. The architecture is clever because it

Below: *In Litchfield National Park, the Lost City is accessible by four-wheel-drive.*

Left: *Tjaynera Falls in Litchfield National Park.* **Above:** *Blyth Homestead, a relic of Litchfield National Park's past.*

allows the termites to regulate the temperature and humidity within their buildings.

Spend some time learning about these mounds and their inhabitants at the information bay provided. Also constructed at the site, a boardwalk provides excellent opportunities for photography especially in the early morning and late afternoon.

Other attractions are Greenant Creek, Tabletop Swamp, the Western Escarpment, Walker Creek and Bamboo Creek Tin Mine. Every one of them is bewitching and each has its own individual appeal. A walk from Greenant Creek takes you through a beautiful rainforest to view Tjaetaba Falls. Tabletop Woodland Forest is a very large thickly wooded flat area where it is always cool and full of enticing shadows. Tabletop Swamp is located about five kilometres north-east of Tolmer Falls and is surrounded by paperbark forest, home for a marvellous variety of wildlife. It is small but exquisite. Despite its size, it is part of the water reservoir for all the major attractions of the park.

Below: *Sugar Gliders are among the myriad of animals in Litchfield National Park.*

Above: *Ferns cascade from the escarpment within Litchfield National Park.*

From Walker Creek carpark you can visit a series of attractive swimming sites and observe the myriad of birds that inhabit the fringing vegetation.

You should not miss Blyth Homestead. Established in 1924—history is indeed young here—the Stapleton pastoral lease was granted as a result of the Commonwealth's need to show something, anything, for its efforts in developing the north.

This was not the only commercial concern in Litchfield. Remains of some alluvial diggings can be found nearby. Until the early 1950s, the park was the site of several tin, tantalite and copper mines and relics of this mining era can be seen today, including Bamboo Creek Tin Mine which ceased operation 25 years ago. Areas near Wangi Falls were explored for uranium in the 1980s. Just outside the park's boundaries near Batchelor is the now rehabilitated site of Rum Jungle Mine, Australia's first uranium mine, which was opened in the 1950s and operated into the 1970s. Permission from the Northern Territory Department of Lands, Planning and Environment needs to be obtained before visiting this site.

There is a rich flora community in the park, including the Darwin Woollybutt and Stringybark, as well as Banksias, Grevilleas, Terminalias and a wide variety of other woodland species. Patches of monsoonal rainforest thrive in the deep, narrow gorges. Species such as the Carpentaria Palm and Umbrella Tree reach to unbelievable heights in search of sunlight. The roots and leaves of a climbing species, *Epipremnum amplissimum*, are used by Aboriginal people for rheumatic pain.

The fauna is equally varied. Common wildlife species include the Antilopine Wallaroo, Agile Wallaby, Sugar Glider, Northern Brushtail Possum, Fawn Antechinus, Black and Little Red Flying Foxes and Dingoes.

Litchfield is a haven for hundreds of native bird species. Black Kites and other birds of prey are common during the Dry season. The Yellow Oriole, Figbird, Koel, Spangled Drongo, Dollarbird and Rainbow Bee-eater inhabit the more sheltered areas near the waterfalls. Rangers at Batchelor can supply lists of flora and fauna on request.

Visitors walking the trails through the monsoon vine-forest may be startled by the enormous size of the impressive but harmless Nephila Spider with its strong sticky web strung between the trees. The black and yellow female of the species can be the size of a human hand while the tiny orange male is barely visible.

Extensive wetlands associated with the Finniss, Daly and Reynolds rivers are vital breeding grounds for waterbird species including the Magpie Goose, and, naturally, are home to Saltwater Crocodiles. Warning signs have been erected in areas known to be inhabited by crocodiles and should never be ignored.

Excellent short walking trails have been established to provide the best possible access to the main features, signs have been erected to give visitors important information about the park, as well as necessary warnings to ensure visitor safety. For long treks, bushwalkers need a permit which can be obtained from the Ranger Station at

Batchelor or from the Parks and Wildlife Commission at Palmerston.

Treat Litchfield as you would a precious heirloom because that it what it is, a valuable possession that must be passed on to future generations.

Urban Parks

The Parks and Wildlife Commission also manages a number of parks and reserves in and around Darwin city.

Botanic Gardens

About two kilometres from the city centre are Darwin's Botanic Gardens. This lush and shady 42-hectare retreat is a significant player in the international network of more than 1500 botanic gardens and is widely acknowledged as one of only a few public gardens within the wet-dry monsoon tropics zone.

There is interesting history behind its establishment which dates to around 1869, when

Below: Darwin's Botanic Gardens, a quiet refuge for locals and visitors.

Darwin was first settled. Basically this was just a vegetable patch, an attempt by the settlers to become self-sufficient in tropical fruits and vegetables because shipping from the south was unreliable.

A German immigrant, Maurice Holtze, was appointed Darwin's first official gardener in 1878. He got to work methodically and with zeal in what is now the suburb of Fannie Bay where he cleared about 12 hectares of scrub, sank wells and planted the area with tropical fruit trees, bananas and arrowroot. In 1886, Holtze engaged a gang of Chinese labourers and began work on the present Darwin Botanic Gardens. In an incredible display of gardening skill, the team transplanted 287 trees from the old gardens and lost only 14 in the process, a feat that would be difficult to emulate even with today's modern techniques.

Holtze departed from Darwin in 1891 leaving the care of the Gardens to his son Nicholas who began the process of importing species of tropical trees from throughout the world. It was patient work and it paid off. Their efforts were completed by those of a remarkable gardener and curator, Jack Agostini, who took on the task of re-establishing the Gardens immediately after the Second World War.

The Botanic Gardens have survived three savage cyclones, in 1897, 1937 and, of course, Cyclone Tracy in 1974 when about 80 per cent of the trees and shrubs were destroyed. Much of what is seen in this peaceful oasis today has been planted since 1974 and it is a fitting tribute to another great gardener, George Brown (now Darwin's Lord Mayor) who joins the list of his distinguished predecessors.

Of more than 2000 species now growing in the gardens, about 400 are palms and plants used traditionally by Top End Aboriginal people for food, medicine, ceremonies, tools, utensils, dyes, fibre and art. The Parks and Wildlife Commission, in co-operation with local Aboriginal people, has established a series of ethno-botanical walking trails through the Gardens to emphasise the crucial importance of native plants to the Aboriginal way of life.

The Gardens feature excellent collections of tropical orchids, bromeliads, ferns, anthuriums, alocasias and heliconias. Exotic tree species include the Raintree, the shallow rooted African Mahogany, and the spectacular Indian Rosewood. Dominant native tree species include the Banyan, Northern Milkwood, and Darwin Black Wattle. Many of these trees are survivors from Maurice Holtze's original plantings.

The Plant Display House contains an excellent range of tropical orchids, ferns, bromeliads and other exotic plants.

Darwin Botanic Gardens is ideal for family picnics, barbecues and other social functions. A large paved area by a lily pond includes electric barbecues, tables and seats. Toilets and playground equipment are also provided. Recent

Below: *Green Tree Frogs are common visitors to Darwin gardens and homes.* **Right:** *Pandanus groves are a feature of Holmes Jungle.*

work in the Gardens has also provided new feature areas including a major fountain and man made lake. Part of a larger plan to develop the Gardens to an international standard, the work will enhance the existing uses of the Gardens.

The Gardens are a definite must in your list of attractions.

Holmes Jungle Nature Park

Holmes Jungle Nature Park is a 250-hectare park off Vanderlin Drive, opposite Karama in Darwin's northern suburbs featuring a remnant monsoon rainforest watered by a permanent spring. Panoramic views of adjacent undulating ridgeland, swampland and tropical woodland can be had from this site which is ideal for picnicking, walking and observing native plants and animals.

Holmes Jungle has a colourful past. It has been a favourite for Darwin residents practically since settlement in 1869 when it was better known as Jungle Creek or Palm Creek. It was named after a turn-of-the-century Darwin businessman, Felix Holmes, who was the town's butcher and first supplier of commercial electricity.

The land was transferred to Holmes by Maurice Holtze mainly for the purpose of agisting cattle that Holmes ran in what is now Nightcliff and Lee Point. During the Second World War, the Army established a convalescent camp there and the site was run down. But it was rehabilitated in the late 1960s and 1970s in a process which involved removing introduced species.

Today Holmes Jungle is protected as a rich and diverse forest habitat containing some distinctive trees like the Banyan and several palm species. Several bird species are found here, including the Rainbow Pitta and the Orange Footed Scrub Fowl. Snakes and lizards, including goannas, are common.

The Parks and Wildlife Commission has established picnic grounds, toilets, parking areas, walking tracks and a scenic lookout.

Howard Springs Nature Park

This 383-hectare park is 35 kilometres from Darwin via the fully sealed Howard Springs Road off the Stuart Highway. It is a deliciously cool, refreshing nature retreat with safe swimming, picnic and barbecue facilities, wildlife watching and interpretive forest walks. Camping is not permitted.

The large natural pool is fed by the Howard River, named after Captain Frederick Howard of HMS Beatrice which, in 1864, carried British settlers to Escape Cliffs on Cape Hotham near the mouth of the Adelaide River. In early days, the area was called Wargan and Freer Springs and did not become known as Howard Springs until 1936.

Early this century, this large supply of fresh water was used for Vestey's Meatworks, a failed large venture on Bullocky Point where Darwin High School stands today. The reliable water supply also attracted the defence forces which, during the Second World War, built a weir at the springs to supplement Darwin's water supplies.

In 1957, Howard Springs became the first northern region nature reserve administered by the then NT Reserves Board, a forerunner to the Parks and Wildlife Commission.

The flora is typical of parts of the Top End and encompasses areas of monsoon forest, open woodland and low-lying swamplands. A dense monsoon forest with luxuriant climbing ferns shades the main swimming pool and creek banks.

The fauna includes more than 250 native animal species, among them 125 birds, 60 reptiles, 22 mammals, 21 fish and 11 amphibians. One bird of particular note is the vibrantly-plumed Rainbow Pitta which might be spotted foraging for snails, worms and insects among the rainforest leaf litter.

Barramundi, Ox-eye Herring, Tarpon and freshwater turtles are common around the main pool area and can be seen from the path across the weir. All animals are protected here and fishing is prohibited.

Casuarina Coastal Reserve

This magnificent 1368-hectare reserve is between Rapid Creek and Lee Point on the edge of Darwin's northern suburbs. Entry to the main beaches is via Trower Road at Brinkin and via Lee Point Road.

The reserve stretches in a wide arc around Darwin's northern waterfront from Rapid Creek to Lee Point and out to sea as far as Old Man Rock, a registered Aboriginal sacred site. It is named after the coastal she-oak which thrives on the foredunes. The park is unquestionably the Territory's most popular park or reserve. An estimated 800,000 visitors and locals are lured every year by its beautiful white beaches,

intriguing marine life and wide variety of land forms and natural habitats.

Box Jellyfish are common in these waters between October and May and visitors are strongly urged not to enter the water at this time.

Casuarina Coastal Reserve is an area of great significance to Aboriginal people. Old Man Rock, clearly visible off Casuarina Beach at low tide, is a particularly important sacred site of the local Larrakia people and should not be disturbed or damaged in any way.

History and geography have not been kind to this coastal area. War-time bunkers to fend off an expected Japanese invasion can still be seen on the beach and cliffs. They were built at considerable damage to this extraordinarily sensitive environment. The beach was sandmined until 1974 when severe storms associated with Cyclone Tracy wreaked further havoc depleting the dune system so badly that the sea almost infiltrated Sandy Creek rainforest in the reserve.

Below: *Casuarina Coastal Reserve's sandstone cliffs reflect the colours of the sun setting over Darwin Harbour.*

Previous Pages: *A water lily breaks the smooth surfaced waters of Manton Dam.* ***Above:*** *Four species of mangroves are found in Casuarina Coastal Reserve.*

However, there has been extensive rehabilitation, stabilisation and regeneration of the entire reserve and, as a result, today it offers a relatively stable habitat for flora and fauna. Four of the Territory's 30 identified mangrove species grow within the reserve, mainly around Rapid Creek and Sandy Creek estuaries. Distinctive Casuarina Trees grow in forest pockets along the foredunes.

The reserve supports one of the most diverse collections of native fauna found anywhere in the Darwin area. Along the coast, majestic Sea Eagles, Whistling Kites and rusty coloured Brahminy Kites glide and swoop in search of food. The mangroves provide a smorgasbord for the Red-headed Honeyeater.

Small mammals, including the Northern Brushtail Possum and Northern Brown Bandicoot thrive within Casuarina's wooded forests. Bats are also common as is a notorious scrounger, the Sand Goanna which may approach humans for a feed.

Marine creatures often seen on or near Casuarina's extensive beaches range in size from the tiny Hermit Crab and Box Jellyfish to large turtles and, occasionally, Dugongs.

The Casuarina bush harbours several snake species of both venomous and non-venomous types. If you see a snake on the track just give it a wide berth.

There are barbecue and picnic facilities, toilets and showers, a surf life-saving club and Darwin's only official 'free beach' for nude bathing. In Darwin's free and easy atmosphere, though, official designations don't seem to have a lot of meaning.

Manton Dam

The 12,900-hectare Manton Dam Recreation Area is off the Stuart Highway 76 kilometres south of Darwin and has become a popular destination for watersports enthusiasts seeking safe refuge from the Box Jellyfish threat in Top End coastal waters during the Wet season.

The dam was built in 1941 to supply fresh water to the city of Darwin and for visiting warships and was opened for watersports in the late 1980s. The NT Power and Water Authority has closed off some areas of this impressive waterway because the dam is still used as a backup for Darwin's water supply in case the Darwin River Dam, which supplies the city today, runs short.

While most people visit Manton Dam Recreation Area to water ski, there are other aspects of the area worth noting. Bushwalkers have plenty of opportunity to observe local wildlife here. The Top End's largest native mammal, the shy Antilopine Wallaroo, is a common sight in the mornings and evenings as it feeds on the lower grassy slopes near the dam.

Fishing enthusiasts should have no trouble hooking a catch from the healthy population of Saratoga which thrive in these waters. And, in the early 1990s, the NT Department of Primary Industry and Fisheries released about 100,000 farm-bred Barramundi fingerlings into Manton Dam in a bid to make fishing even more attractive for visitors in the future. The fingerlings take some two years to mature and reach the 55 centimetre legal catch size for Barramundi.

Manton Dam is a pleasant destination for day trippers out of Darwin and offers good picnic and barbecue facilities as well as plenty of shady, grassed areas to relax. There are clear boundaries between the different user zones, and these must be strictly observed for the sake of public safety.

Territory Wildlife Park

Totalling 805 hectares, the Territory Wildlife Park is off the Cox Peninsula Road, 67 kilometres south of Darwin and features the world's most comprehensive collection of Northern Territory wildlife species. The adjoining Berry Springs Nature Park complements the Wildlife Park with its excellent and safe swimming, walking and picnicking facilities.

Officially opened in 1990, planning for the Territory Wildlife Park began almost immediately after self-government in 1978. The site was selected by then Taronga Park Zoo Director, Dr P. Crowcroft, in 1979. It is an ideal site because it includes diverse natural habitats, a varied landscape, plentiful natural water supply and soils suitable for economic construction work.

Development began in June 1984 and the virgin bush site at Berry Springs was carefully transformed into Australia's most innovative wildlife park—the Territory's first such facility.

It boasts one of the most comprehensive and valuable wildlife collections in Australia, including species not found in zoological gardens anywhere else in the world.

This is the only zoological institution in Australia which nominates research and conservation as its major objective. It has won international acclaim for its commitment to wildlife conservation and for its ongoing efforts to save some of Australia's most threatened species. Its highly successful captive breeding program includes several world firsts.

Visitors may walk or ride a shuttle train on a four kilometre ring-road to experience a fascinating journey to see Territory wildlife in a variety of natural habitats. Among the attractions are a twice daily display of some of the park's birds of prey in flight, an animal care centre, a

Below: *The Territory Wildlife Park's aquarium provides an underwater view of a Top End billabong.*

bird hide from which to watch thousands of birds attracted to the park's Goose Lagoon, and well constructed walkways through monsoon forest.

An aquarium gives visitors an underwater view of a typical Top End billabong via a large walk-through acrylic tunnel. Turtles, fish and stingrays and a large saltwater crocodile can be seen, at close quarters. A walk-through aviary includes a huge mesh dome, while a nocturnal house allows visitors to see some of the Territory's nocturnal animals by simulating a night environment inside the house.

It will be readily obvious why this park is an award winner and a full day should be allowed to see all that it has to offer.

Berry Springs Nature Park

Berry Springs Nature Park is adjacent to the Territory Wildlife Park. This has long been a popular weekend recreational retreat for Darwin families and visitors. It is the perfect place to relax and enjoy a refreshing swim and barbecue.

The park area was the site of a Second World War convalescent and rest-and-recreation camp, and the weir across Berry Creek was built during the war years.

Berry Springs Nature Park features extensive lawn and shady areas, a superb freshwater swimming hole and monsoon rainforest. Barbecues and toilets are provided.

Berry Creek's lower reaches are brackish and surrounded by monsoon forest but this area is inhabited by saltwater crcodiles and is not accessible to visitors. The upper reaches remain free of saltwater intrusion because of the flushing effect of freshwater springs discharging into Berry Creek.

Left: Birds of prey like this Wedge-tailed Eagle provide a spectacular display with their handlers at the Territory Wildlife Park. *Below:* Near the Territory Wildlife Park, Berry Springs Nature Park provides an ideal spot for a picnic and paddle to cool off.

Tiwi Islands

Melville and Bathurst Islands are twin jewels just north of Darwin. They are the home of the Tiwi, a proud Aboriginal people perhaps best known nationally for the unending stream of champion Australian Rules Football players they seem to spawn.

The islands are only a short flight from Darwin, but a world away from the mainland all the same. Here you sniff the first pungent aroma of Asia and feel its exotic life. But last century these remarkable people managed to fend off all comers—Macassan, Dutch and British—to maintain a kind of sturdy independence.

The Tiwi face the future just as they confronted the past, unafraid. That is not a bad outcome for more than 200 years of sometimes bloody contact with outsiders.

Both islands unfold sinuously as you fly in, hundreds of white beaches crowned by dense forest and devoid of any sign of human habitation.

Here, as elsewhere, the Aboriginal people believe in a single act of creation for the islands. The story about Mudungkala, a legendary human being who created the islands, explains it. She was an old blind woman who arose from the ground carrying three babies in her arms. There was nothing in the landscape, just a darkened and barren piece of earth. But as she crawled she carved a narrow channel between Bathurst and Melville Islands and the darkness filled with seawater and plants and animals. The narrow channel, Apsley Strait, is subject to huge tidal forces.

Before Mudungkala went back into the ground, she had created paradise for her children, a land abundant with goods and a blue sparkling sea where fish almost leapt into canoes. No one could have asked for more. But as with other legends for people around the globe, paradise was not enough. It seems that human nature intruded to spoil it.

One of Mudungkala's children, Purukupali, fought the Moon Man, Tjapara, with forked sticks creating another legend that later would inspire the superb Tiwi carvings and designs, in particular the Tiwi burial poles. Known as Pukamani burial poles, they are a unique feature of Tiwi funeral ceremonies. Specially carved and decorated, a number of poles are planted in the ground to mark a grave site and include symbolic designs.

Mudungkala's descendants form special groups called Imunga. They are fairly similar to, for example Scottish clans, except that here clan groupings are passed from the mother, not the father. Owning land, on the other hand, is patrilineal. The parallel system appears to work well. Cultural and social affairs are controlled by women while economic affairs are the responsibility of men.

The plane from Darwin may land at Pickertaramoor, a small strip in the southern part of Melville Island servicing a sprawling pine plantation. This is a charming cluster of old forestry homes encircled by old growth rainforest. Nearby is a beautiful waterfall and picnic grounds set amidst riotous vegetation. A little beyond, the pine plantation begins. The trees have come a long way, mainly from the torrid Caribbean, and have adapted to their new home well. The plantation, a tourist attraction in itself, provides income to the Tiwi.

About 40 kilometres from Pickertaramoor is Taracumbie Falls which often feature in advertisements for the islands. This is a place of tranquility and beauty. Clear waters tumble among rocks after a brief struggle with ancient and huge tree roots and exotic ferns.

The falls are on land that belongs to a well known Territory family, the Tipilouras who are all members of the Wulirangkuwu clan. One of the

Left: The Vernon Islands can be seen on the flight to the Tiwi Islands.

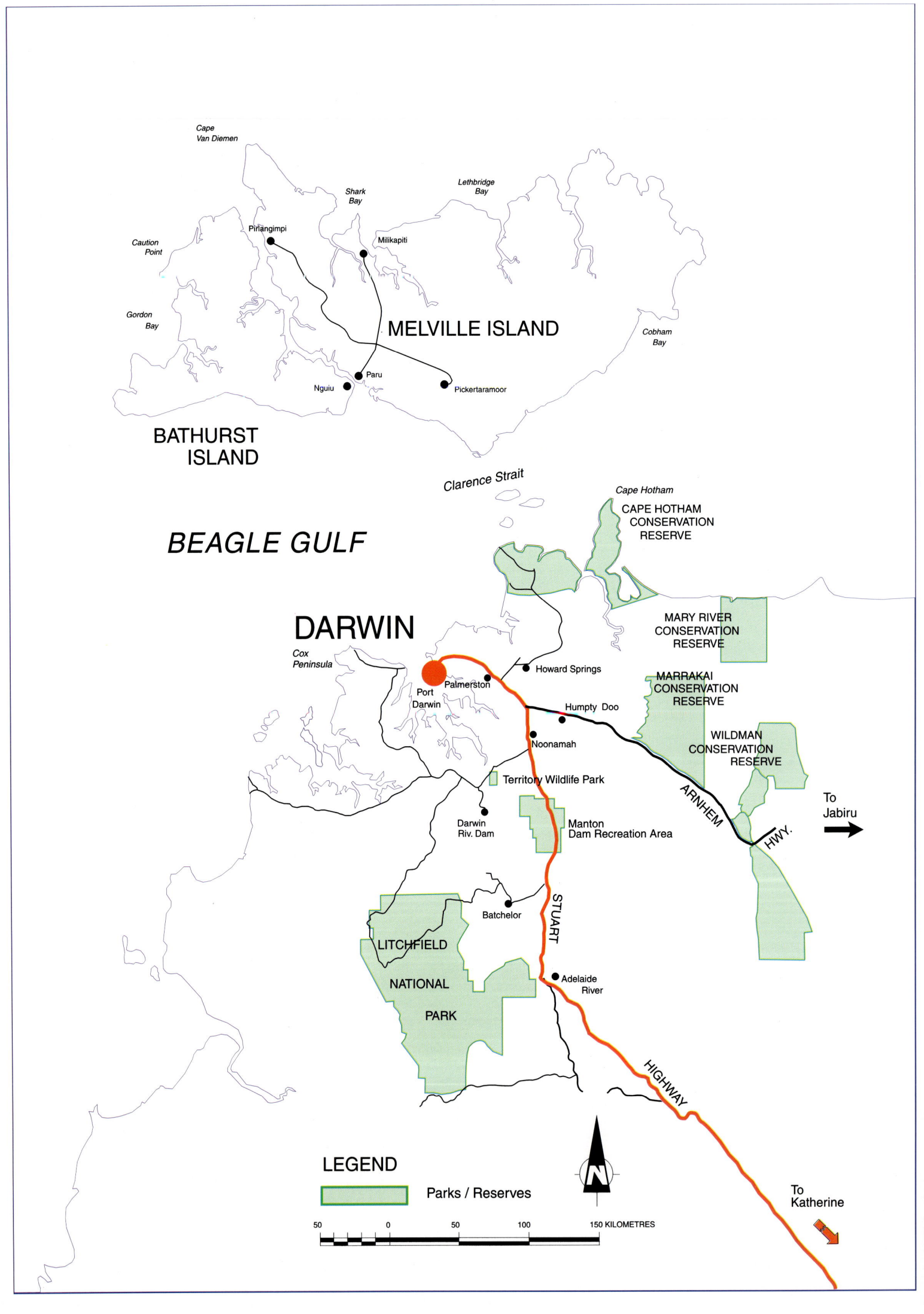

Cape
Van Diemen

Shark
Bay

Lethbridge
Bay

Pirlangimpi

Milikapiti

Caution
Point

MELVILLE ISLAND

Cobham
Bay

Gordon
Bay

Paru

Nguiu

Pickertaramoor

BATHURST
ISLAND

Clarence Strait

Cape Hotham

CAPE HOTHAM
CONSERVATION
RESERVE

BEAGLE GULF

MARY RIVER
CONSERVATION
RESERVE

DARWIN

MARRAKAI
CONSERVATION
RESERVE

Cox
Peninsula

Palmerston

Howard Springs

Port
Darwin

Humpty Doo

WILDMAN
CONSERVATION
RESERVE

Noonamah

Territory Wildlife Park

ARNHEM

To Jabiru

HWY.

Darwin
Riv. Dam

Manton
Dam Recreation Area

STUART

Batchelor

LITCHFIELD

Adelaide
River

NATIONAL

PARK

HIGHWAY

LEGEND

N

Parks / Reserves

To
Katherine

50   0   50   100   150 KILOMETRES

Tipilouras, Stan, was a distinguished Territory parliamentarian who died relatively recently. Bernard Tipiloura was for a long time a member of the Parks and Wildlife Commission, and Bob Collins, a Federal Government politician, is married into the Tipiloura family.

From the falls it is only a short side trip to the Tiwi burial sites of Milikapiti (Snake Bay) and its fantastic collection of burial poles. Many of the designs on the poles are truly carving masterpieces giving visitors a clear example of the Tiwi's artistic abilities. Certainly Tiwi designs, traditionally used on ceremonial objects, have gained international reputation and are helping build a burgeoning industry on the islands.

Milikapiti is an impressive bay stretching seemingly forever and includes coves, beaches, forests and cliffs which are a feast for the eyes. This is a monster harbour, practically unvisited and pristine.

The road from Milikapiti to Pirlangimpi takes you through imposing pine plantations. A couple of creeks on the way hold small forests of Nipa Palms which probably originated in Papua New Guinea and do not exist anywhere else in Australia.

Pirlangimpi, formerly called Pularumpi, is well worth visiting for at least three reasons: it has an exquisite shoreline, it is the home of some of Australia's best know football players and, nearby, are the ruins of Britain's attempt to establish its first settlement in northern Australia.

The beaches are magnificent and inviting. They are also untouched by development of almost any kind and remain as wild and untamed as they have been for thousands of years. This is virgin country. As far as the eye can see, the sand, sea and bush combine to give jaded refugees from the industrial world a rest from it all. You cannot get much further away from the smog and noise of the city than this.

When you arrive you may be greeted by a group of youngsters playing football. That is because Australian Rules Football is almost as important to these people as the Catholic Church. The code is a religion for the Tiwi and has been institutionalised by the likes of Cyril Rioli, the grand old man of football, whose neat cottage at Pirlangimpi is full of trophies won in the 'south'. The annual football fixture at Bathurst has become a classic Territory event attended by people from all over Australia.

Finally, this place has some glorious history as well. Across a small bay overlooking Apsley Strait there is a heavily wooded promontory which looks inoffensive enough. In fact, the forested hillock is the site of Fort Dundas, a place of hell for Captain Gordon Bremer of the Royal Navy and his people who, in 1824, attempted to establish a settlement there. He arrived on the warship Tamar accompanied by the vessels Countess of Harcourt and Lady Nelson with a handful of troops and crew. Captain Bremer and the Colonial Office

Below: *Burial poles are found on Karslake Peninsula.* **Overleaf:** *Taracumbie Falls on Melville Island.*

which had sent him there hoped the port would become a great entrepot for the East Indian Archipelago, but it was not a good site for a sea port. Treacherous seas blocked the southern entrance to the strait and, to make matters worse, the fort was built in November 1824, right at the start of the Wet season which that year was very wet indeed. Rain made life miserable for the settlers. The brig Lady Nelson was lost at sea in early 1825 and another supply ship, the Stedcombe, was taken by pirates and plundered. Of the crew, only two boys were spared, the rest killed.

Relations between the proud Tiwi and the settlers were not good. Clashes and skirmishes were almost continuous and while the Tiwi showed a healthy regard for firearms this did not stop encounters with newcomers. Many became sick making their lot even more miserable.

Fort Dundas was abandoned in March 1829. Its melancholy ruins, surrounded by a moat, are now almost totally covered by the jungle. Next to nothing remains of the few structures they built except some small piles of rocks and a pervading sense of hopelessness and futility.

Below: *Wild Ginger grows on the site of Fort Dundas.*

Above: *Milikapiti (Snake Bay) on Melville Island.*

War returned with a thump in February 1942 when the Japanese bombed the islands on their way to Darwin. The large flight of 188 planes was first detected by John Gribble, a navy coastwatcher manning a post on the northern tip of Melville Island at 9.15am February 19, 1942. Twenty minutes later, Father John McGrath, a Catholic missionary reported an unusually large number of aircraft bearing down on the mission from the north west. The aircraft strafed the mission. Both men duly reported their sighting to the authorities in Darwin who ignored their desperate message.

A Tiwi, Mathias Ulungara, captured a Japanese pilot who crash landed on Melville Island, the only Japanese captured on Australian soil. The pilot would later feature prominently in the infamous Cowra breakout.

The islands therefore are not just precious natural gems, they are ancient repositories of history.

The islanders are receptive to economic development and have begun to make a timid entry into tourism. The Barra Lodge, on Bathurst Island, is an attractive lodge which combines comfort with the ruggedness of bush life. Placed on the beach, it offers visitors the rare spectacle of saltwater crocodiles coming onto the sand to be fed.

At some stage, the Tiwi Islands are bound to be discovered by people who have seen it all and are looking for something different. At present, a small airline offers one-day tours daily (except Sunday) or two-day tours (except Sunday and Monday) from Darwin.

The islands are Aboriginal land under the administration of the Tiwi Land Council established in 1977. A permit is needed to gain access but the process is not difficult and the friendly islanders welcome visitors. All they ask is that, in turn, their traditions and the land that is their home are treated with respect.

Below: *Forestry provides an income for islanders.* **Overleaf:** *Sunset shows the Northern Territory's tropical delights.*

Index

Published by New Holland Publishers Pty Ltd
3/2 Aquatic Drive, Frenchs Forest, NSW 2086, Australia

Devised by the Parks and Wildlife Commission of the Northern Territory

First edition 1989
Second edition 1992
Third edition 1994, reprinted 1995
Fully revised edition 1996

National Library Cataloguing-in-Publication data

Alcorta, Frank.
Explore Australia's Northern Territory.

Rev. ed.
Includes index.

ISBN 1 86436 240 5.

1. National parks and reserves—Northern Territory.
2. Northern Territory—Description and travel—1976-1990
I. Title.

919.4290463

Reproduction by DNL Resources Pty Ltd
Printed and bound by Kyodo Printing Co (Pte) Ltd, Singapore

Cover photograph: *The magnificent Twin Falls in Kakadu National Park dwarfs a helicopter.*

Photographic acknowledgements:
K Atkinson: *pages 14 (bottom), 31, 108, 138, 172* **S Churchill**: *101* **D Evans**: *96-97, 151 (bottom), 153, 156-157,*
159, 167, 170, 171 (top), 180 **T Forde**: *184, 186 (top and bottom), 187, 188-189* **M Gillam**: *66-67* **A Ginns**: *34-35,*
62 (top), 64, 74 **D Hancock**: *26-27, 75, 79 (bottom), 80 (top), 82, 84-85, 90, 91 (top), 105, 106 (top and bottom),*
112 (top), 113 (bottom), 114-115, 118-119, 121 (bottom), 122-123, 129-131, 133-135, 141, 144-147, 173, 175-177,
192 **P Jarver**: *95, 158* **K Johnson**: *51* **A Julius**: *48-49, 52, 124-125, 163* **V Lockley**: *100* **A Mathieson**: *86-87*
A McGregor: *126* **I Morris**: *91 (bottom), 132 (bottom), 136 (top)* **Northern Territory Tourist Commission**: *11*
(bottom) **Parks and Wildlife Commission**: *19, 70-71, 80 (bottom), 81, 113 (top), 116, 120 (top), 121 (top), 148,*
162, 164, 165 (bottom), 166, 178-179, 183 **A Pickering**: *83 (bottom), 110-111* **D Roff**: *xii, 2-3, 4 (top and bottom),*
5 (top, middle and bottom), 6-7, 11 (top), 14 (top), 16 (bottom) 17, 20-21, 23 (bottom), 28, 34, 35 (top and bottom),
40, 41 (bottom), 42-44, 46 (top and bottom), 52, 55, 56 (top and bottom), 63, 65 (bottom), 68, 69 (top and bottom),
72-73, 132 (top), 136 (bottom), 137, 168, back cover (bottom) **T Sandery**: *8, 16 (top), 22, 23 (top), 24-25*
D Shultz: *107 (top)* **S Strike**: *back cover (top)* **VA Thomas**: *152 (top)* **P Timney**: *120 (bottom)* **T Vigus**: *160-161*
F Woerle: *front cover, 10-13, 15, 18, 36-39, 41 (top), 45, 47, 58-61, 62 (bottom), 76, 79 (top), 83 (top), 88-89, 92-94,*
98-99, 102, 107 (bottom), 109, 112 (bottom), 117, 142-143, 149 (top and bottom), 150 (top and bottom), 151 (top),
152 (bottom), 154-155, 165 (top), 169 (top and bottom), 171 (bottom), 174, 181, 182.